Internal audit in the public sector

Internal audit in the public sector

Roger Buttery, *Deputy County Treasurer,*
Lincolnshire County Council
and
Robert K. Simpson, *Controller of Audit,*
Commission for Local Authority Accounts in Scotland

Woodhead-Faulkner · Cambridge

Published by Woodhead-Faulkner Ltd
Fitzwilliam House, 32 Trumpington Street, Cambridge CB2 1QY, England
and 51 Washington Street, Dover, NH 03820, USA

First published 1986

British Library Cataloguing in Publication Data
Buttery, Roger.
Internal audit in the public sector.
1. Finance, Public—Great Britain—Accounting 2. Auditing, internal—Great Britain
I. Title II. Simpson, Robert K
657′.8350458 HJ9925.G6

ISBN 0-85941-262-8
ISBN 0-85941-272-5 Pbk

Library of Congress Cataloging in Publication Data
Buttery, Roger.
Internal audit in the public sector.

Includes index.
1. Auditing, internal. 2. Finance, public—Accounting.
3. Management audit. I. Simpson, Robert K. II. Title.
HF5668.25.B87 1985 657′.8350458 85-5330

ISBN 0-85941-262-8
ISBN 0-85941-272-5 (pbk.)

Designed by Ron Jones

Typeset by Hands Fotoset, Leicester

Printed in Great Britain by St Edmundsbury Press, Bury St Edmunds, Suffolk

Contents

Preface

The purpose of this book is to provide, under one cover, a concise but comprehensive guide to the principles and practical problems of internal audit in the public sector. The book is aimed at both students and practitioners in all public sector organisations. Reference is also made to external audit, so public sector external auditors will find it a useful reference book.

The public sector almost defies definition since its boundaries vary according to the criteria by which one wishes to delineate it. It may or may not include, according to one's definition, the trading activities of 'public' bodies, some public corporations, the 'privatised' provision of public services and government grants to private industry. In the context of auditing, it is arguably more useful to avoid equivocal definitions of what constitutes the public sector, and to concentrate instead on identifying features which distinguish it from the private sector. These would include the following, to varying extents:

1. The public ownership of assets or trusteeships on behalf of the nation or a locality.
2. The accountability to Parliament or a local authority electorate.
3. Public expectations for, and the rigorous application of, the concept of integrity in public service (although it is frequently equally expected of individuals in the private sector as well).
4. The impact on internal control of the absence of a profit motive.
5. Material financial support from the Exchequer or rates and precepts.
6. The commissioning or production of public goods.
7. The inoperability in some bodies of certain accounting concepts, e.g. going concern basis and accruals concept.
8. The inoperability in some bodies of certain financial yardsticks, e.g. liquidity ratios, rate of return on capital and gearing.
9. The comparative absence of competition, particularly in monopolies.

The list is not intended to be exhaustive, but the presence of one or more of such factors raises issues which the auditor would do well to bear in mind when examining the activities and financial affairs of a public sector body. Special considerations could apply in planning such an audit which might not assume the same importance in a private sector audit. The most obvious example is value-for-money examinations.

Throughout the book, our aim has been to produce concise information on the full range of matters affecting internal audit in the public sector, covering such issues as its role and objectives, auditing standards, audit management, audit documentation, conduct of an audit, fraud and corruption, value for money, specialist areas such as contract and computer audit and national developments. In view of the nature of this publication, references to audit techniques and particular types of audit have been kept to a minimum, although the principal techniques are identified and examples are provided of internal control questionnaires and audit programmes.

From time to time, the book draws on the work undertaken by the Chartered Institute of Public Finance and Accountancy (CIPFA), and we are grateful to this Institute for allowing us this facility.

September 1985

Roger Buttery
Robert K. Simpson

CHAPTER 1

The role and objectives of internal audit

Introduction

Internal audit is an integral part of the financial structure of public authorities. Most public authorities recognised the importance of internal audit many years ago, some of the larger ones adopting it in the early years of this century, and today very few, if any, public authorities operate without some form of internal audit. Over the years, however, the precise role of internal audit has changed. In the early days, its primary responsibility was concerned with the detection and prevention of errors and fraud, with perhaps an overdue concentration on examining accounts before payment, collecting income and checking petty cash claims. Today, internal audit operates in a more dynamic environment with an emphasis on reviewing systems of internal control. Internal audit exists within public authorities to carry out an independent appraisal of the effectiveness of internal controls, financial and other, operating within each organisation.

Definition

Over the years, various bodies/persons have produced statements on, and definitions of, the role and objectives of internal audit. For the purpose of this book, the 'role and objectives' statement, published by the Chartered Institute of Public Finance and Accountancy (CIPFA), has been used. CIPFA is one of the six major professional accountancy bodies in the United Kingdom and is the premier body which specialises in financial management for public sector bodies. (The complete 'role and objectives' statement is reproduced in Appendix 1.)

Internal audit and internal control

In the authors' view, there is only one working definition of internal audit and that is that it is an independent appraisal function within an organisation for the review of activities as a service to all levels of management. Regrettably, the 'independent appraisal function' has not been accepted by all public sector organisations, particularly certain areas of local government and the health service. For example, some organisations do not have separate internal audit sections engaged solely on audit duties. In this situation, internal audit is part of the departmental systems and procedures, which means a consequential loss in audit's effectiveness. Some internal audit sections, for example, are responsible for monitoring the regularity of banking, administering car loans or checking every pension benefit. This is a complete misuse of internal audit's resources.

One of the reasons for this state of affairs is that there is confusion over internal audit and internal control. Internal control is quite clearly management's responsibility, in order that its activities are conducted in an efficient and well-ordered manner. Internal audit is not a substitute for good management and it is in this area that misunderstandings have arisen. Consequently, the chief architect of a public sector organisation is responsible for the whole system of financial and other controls which is established within his department to safeguard its assets, ensure reliability of records, promote operational efficiency and monitor adherence to policies and objectives. For example, the controls might include a time-recording/costing system for the design staff. It is not internal audit's job to implement and operate such a system, it is the responsibility of the chief architect. Similarly, a director of housing in a local authority is responsible for the whole range of systems within the housing department which should include the utilisation of houses. Again, it is not internal audit's responsibility to implement and operate such a system but it is that of the director of housing.

In the past, and even today in some organisations, internal audit still works to narrow terms of reference and continues to concentrate on appraising, for example, the accuracy of income and petty cash and the propriety of creditors. Whilst this aspect will always be an important feature of the control function, it must not be allowed to dominate internal audit's activities. Internal audit's responsibilities are much wider and, as an absolute minimum, it is essential that the principal internal control systems are properly appraised and that a report on their effectiveness is made to management.

Independence

For a public sector organisation to achieve the maximum benefit from the activities of internal audit, it is essential that the auditor should not be engaged in any system which he would normally review and appraise.

Internal audit activity should be unrestricted and auditors should have full rights of access to records, assets and personnel, and should receive such information and explanations as they consider necessary for the performance of their duties. (The whole question of independence is discussed in Chapter 3.)

CHAPTER 2
Auditing standards

We live in an era of standards. It seems that every professional and quasi-professional body, in every discipline in every sector, is seeking to impose its will upon the world in the form of standards. Audit is no exception to this and the auditor is faced with a bewildering selection of standards, covering both the ethical and the operational aspects of his work. Most professional bodies issue a code of ethics and it is not the purpose of this chapter to question or even to examine these, but to examine the general and operational standards that apply to auditors working in the public sector.

What are 'standards'? The dictionary defines a standard as 'an exemplary model, measure of quality or value, a target of excellence to be attained, an agreed, universal principle'. And what are internal audit standards? Recourse to the dictionary provides us with four subtly different explanations of the meaning of 'standard' in the context of internal auditing, as follows:

1. An authoritative, recognised exemplar of correctness, or perfection.
2. A definite level of excellence, a definite measure of what is adequate, a prescribed object of endeavour.
3. A criterion, goal or yardstick against which performance is judged.
4. An agreed norm or universally applicable principle.

It can be observed that the last two definitions are value-free, implying no set level of prescription; however, the first two imply a prescribed level, be it of adequacy or excellence. A further sense can also be discerned – that of 'consistency'.

Four issues emerge from these considerations, as follows:

1. At what *level* should standards be set – minimum, adequate, acceptable, high or optimum?
2. Do standards imply 'standardisation', or is this to confuse consistency with uniformity?
3. Can standards be universally applicable? How can they be appropriate to all organisations in all situations?
4. What *are* the fundamental principles of internal auditing? What is 'internal auditing as it should be' and who says what it should be?

The need for internal audit standards

It can be contended that many would benefit from the promulgation and application of standards – the professions, practising auditors, the client and society. Various pressures led to their development – allegations of poor standards (in practice) of audit (external and internal), reviews of existing practice, a desire for conformity with others, the striving for 'professionalism', a fear of external control and the perceived need for self-regulation.

Many specific objectives and benefits of internal auditing standards can be put forward. They are as follows:

1. To define an acceptable standard.
2. To establish a basis for guidance for auditors, old and new.
3. To determine responsibilities for those with a duty, both to provide and operate an effective internal audit unit.
4. To act as yardsticks and measures of competence.
5. To demonstrate professionalism and a sense of responsibility, thus enhancing credibility, providing assurance and ensuring use of audit's service.
6. To provide publicity for and education concerning the role of internal audit.
7. To promote consistency and reliability.
8. To provoke change in others.
9. To codify best principles and best practice.
10. To enable comparison.
11. To stimulate debate or review.
12. To unite the internal audit community.
13. To improve self-confidence.
14. To improve performance.

Those supporting the publication of standards point to three main benefits – acceptance of internal audit, a better sense of purpose and better internal auditing.

Production of standards

Until very recently, there were no published standards for internal audit in the public sector, and existing practice was based on a variety of guidelines which came from a number of sources. Even at the time of writing, there are no standards for internal audit in the public sector recognised by the Consultative Committee of Accountancy Bodies (CCAB). However, there have been developments in the last five years and three sets of internal auditing standards have been published, namely: *Statements on Internal Audit Practice – Public Sector* by CIPFA, *Standards for the Professional Practice of Internal Auditing* by the Institute of Internal Auditors, and *Standards for Government Internal Audit* by HM Treasury.

It is fair to say that CIPFA was the first on the scene as its publication appeared in 1979. The CCAB would not allow CIPFA to use the term 'standards' and, whilst the statements were not issued as an enforceable code, they have been adopted by most directors of finance and internal audit managers in the public sector.

CIPFA's statements on internal audit practice

Against a background of concern at the ineffectiveness of many internal audit sections, CIPFA decided there was a need to develop certain standards of internal audit. The CIPFA statements were therefore produced in recognition of the need to promote the establishment of high professional standards of internal audit practice throughout the public sector.

By compiling statements for auditors and those responsible for the internal audit function, it was possible to codify the basic factors contained in existing material to form one source against which future performance could be judged. For the first time, the operation and conduct of the internal audit function in the public sector has been set down for the use of all organisations.

The principles enunciated in the statements are intended to apply to all internal audits conducted by all public sector organisations, irrespective of their size. The statements prescribe basic principles and practices which should be followed in the conduct of all internal audits where the auditor is called upon to express an opinion upon the soundness, adequacy and application of internal control, and to report independently thereon.

The CIPFA statements have been classified under the following two main headings:

1. *General*. This pertains to audit philosophy and principles.
2. *Operational*. This embraces matters directly concerned with internal audit practice, covering scope of audit, audit management, reporting and relationships.

Each statement is divided into two parts – the *statement* (which defines the prime objectives) and an *explanation* (which gives guidance on its application).

The various statements are as follows:

1. The 'role and objectives' statement.
2. General statements on independence and due professional care.
3. Operational statements:
   (*a*) Scope of internal audit.
      Internal control.
      Irregularities and fraud.
   (*b*) Internal audit management.
      Planning and control.
      Supervision.
      Training.
   (*c*) Internal audit reporting.
      Evidence.
      Reporting.
   (*d*) Internal audit relationships.
      External audit.
      Client departments.
      Other review agencies.

As can be seen from these headings, the subjects covered by the statements are dealt with in some depth in the various chapters of this book. It is not necessary, therefore, to deal with each statement in any detail in this chapter; however, all the statements are reproduced for information in Appendix 1.

Implementation

It must be recognised that standards in themselves achieve very little. They are, at most, a catalogue of best practice. Standards must be implemented after they have been produced. To be effective, they must be adopted by audit management and widely publicised and distributed amongst staff, and, most important of all, compliance with them must be closely monitored as an integral part of quality control.

CHAPTER 3

The organisation of internal audit

Independence of audit

Much has been said in the past about the independence of audit and, in many ways, this has proved to be an area of extreme controversy. It has often been seen as the audit manager's bid for chief official status. Whilst independence is considered to be a fundamental principle of audit, without which the audit function would be rendered ineffective, it is not advocated that the audit manager should be a chief officer in his own right. In fact, it is the very benefits of being attached to a department (generally the finance department) which enable the internal audit manager to fulfil his role properly. The audit manager needs the 'tap root' into the system of communication (official and unofficial) which his departmental links provide. Without these links he would become cut off from the organisation which he seeks to help to control.

The independence for the internal audit stems not from departmental independence but from the *independence* of the following:

1. Scope.
2. Access.
3. Report.
4. Activity.
5. Personnel.
6. Mind.

Let us examine these in turn.

Independence of scope

The scope of the auditor's work should not be restricted in any way. He should be free to examine and report upon the activities of any department and any part of any department within the organisation. Obviously, his attention should be drawn to delicate issues and sensitive areas and he must have regard to these in formulating his work programmes; nevertheless, the decision to include or exclude an area of activity should rest with the audit manager and should not be taken by anyone with a direct or indirect vested interest.

Independence of access

In order to carry out his task fully, the auditor must have an unchallengeable right of access at all reasonable times to all financial and associated records of the organisation. He must have the right to examine all assets, including land and buildings, stocks and stores, investment certificates, transport and plant, furniture and fittings and cash. He must be able to require any explanations from any employees that he deems necessary.

Independence of report

The audit manager should be able to report, both verbally and in writing, to all levels of the organisation. Equally important is a direct line of communication to the chief executive which will greatly enhance the impact, and thus the effectiveness, of the audit function.

Independence of activity

This is the area in which so many audit sections fall short of the ideal. Auditors should never become involved in the operation of any system upon which they will ultimately be required to report. Since auditors should be able to report upon any aspect of financial or management control, it follows that they should never become involved in any such activities. Nevertheless, it is quite common to find audit sections involved in controlling financial stationery (cheques, receipts, tickets, etc.), clearing receipting machines, processing invoices for payment, designing financial systems and in many other ways becoming directly involved in systems which they should be responsible for reviewing. Quite often such involvement is because of an emergency, such as staff shortages and peaks of work. Some directors of finance still see audit as an 'available pool of labour' which can readily be called upon to assist in such emergencies, however much that might compromise audit's independence. In the recent past, it became fashionable to combine audit with other activities, such as accounting, to form joint sections. Fortunately, this practice has virtually died out because of the conflict of interests which it created and also, predictably, because audit work took second place to the activity with which it was linked, since that activity inevitably had externally imposed deadlines.

Independence of personnel

This aspect of the concept of audit independence is less easy to arrange in practice, and, the smaller the organisation, the more difficult it becomes. Often the audit manager will have to make the best arrangements he can within the constraints imposed upon him. The ideal which he seeks to achieve is that the audit staff are totally independent of the staff who operate the systems under review. Audit staff should not be required to examine and report upon work done by persons with whom they are related or with whom they have a personal relationship. Similarly, audit staff should not be asked to audit an area of activity in which they themselves have had line management responsibility in the past.

Independence of mind

The independence of mind of the auditor is perhaps the single factor which can exert the greatest impact upon the independence of the audit function. Paradoxically, it is the most difficult to define or measure. The section on recruitment and training (pages 12–16) defines certain qualities which an auditor needs to possess, and perhaps it would have been useful to have included independence of mind in the list. Of course, that would have raised the question of how one tests 'independence of mind' when recruiting staff, and, apart from selective analysis, this is not possible. Many pressures can deflect the auditor from his objective, and it is his independence of mind which serves to protect him from these. Perhaps it can be best described as a quality which incorporates 'single-mindedness', tempered by a cautious awareness of the views of others.

The audit manager

The post of audit manager (or chief internal auditor) is an important one in any public sector organisation. It must be of a sufficient status to command respect throughout the organisation. In a book of this nature, it is not possible to be specific about this status. For one reason, the precise location of internal audit may vary between organisations. For example, in local government, internal audit is usually located in the finance department and the audit manager is responsible to the treasurer or director of finance who has a statutory duty for the provision of internal audit. A similar arrangement exists in the health and water authorities. In other public sector organisations, however, whilst internal audit may be situated in the finance department under the director of finance, the audit manager normally reports, in practice, to the board member for finance.

The post of audit manager carries a great deal of managerial responsibility and requires making many decisions without the need to refer operational problems to a higher authority. It also involves contact and discussion, sometimes critical, with high-ranking officers of other departments and, on occasions, with board members. It is essential that the duties and responsibilities of the post are clearly defined. A typical job description of an audit manager or chief internal auditor is set out as follows:

Job description

Chief internal auditor in the public sector

1. Management responsibilities

The chief internal auditor will be responsible for managing a highly qualified internal audit section comprising the following:

(a) Qualified staff.
(b) Part-qualified staff.
(c) Unqualified staff and trainees.

He will be responsible for their recruitment and for organising a proper training programme involving a co-ordinated use of external courses and 'in-house' training.

2. Objectives

The objectives of internal audit are contained in financial regulations and are consistent with the CIPFA 'role and objectives of internal audit' statement and are embodied in the *Statements on Internal Audit Practice – Public Sector.* The chief internal auditor will be responsible for ensuring that these objectives are achieved.

3. Planning and supervision

The chief internal auditor will be required, at intervals not to exceed three years, to prepare a long-term audit plan, reconciling the staff resources available with the audit tasks to be completed and identifying the main areas of risk. The long-term plan will be submitted to (see footnote 1) for approval and will be kept constantly under review.

The chief internal auditor will also complete an annual detailed plan which he will be required to co-ordinate with that of the external auditor. This plan also will be submitted to (see footnote 1) for approval.

The chief internal auditor will arrange for the proper supervision and review of audit work and will ensure that the agreed audit plan is adhered to.

4. Reporting

The chief internal auditor will be responsible to (see footnote 2) but will have the facility to report under his own name on any matter connected with the organisation to any person within the organisation. Copies of all reports have to be submitted to (see footnote 2).

The chief internal auditor will prepare an annual report on the progress and activities of the internal audit section and this will have to be submitted to (see footnote 3) by a specified date.

5. Relationships

The chief internal auditor will be responsible for ensuring that good working relationships are established and maintained with all executive and central support departments. In particular, he will ensure that a positive response is forthcoming in respect of matters raised by his section.

The chief internal auditor will also ensure that proper lines of communication are maintained with other review agencies such as external audit and management services, in order to avoid duplication and to maximise the use of resources.

The chief internal auditor will maintain close links with the police and will be responsible for referring all frauds and irregularities, after consultation with appropriate officers.

6. Professional responsibility

The chief internal auditor will be required to keep up to date on legislation changes and developments within the auditing profession. He will ensure that his staff are apprised of all relevant changes.

Footnote 1 The person to whom the audit plans are submitted will depend upon the specific management structure. It may be to the director of finance, to the chief executive or to a board member.

Footnote 2 Ideally, the chief internal auditor should be responsible to the director of finance, to the chief executive or to a board member and copies of all reports should be submitted to that person.

Footnote 3 The annual report will normally be submitted to the person to whom the chief internal auditor is responsible. However, it would also be advantageous to supply copies to the finance committee or to the board.

Sizes of audit section

Very little guidance is available to the audit manager to assist him to determine how large his section should be. This is really not surprising since there are so many variables as to make such guidance impossible to produce, except in the broadest of terms. The following is a list of just some of the variables which must be taken into account in fixing the size of a section.

1. *The role of the audit section.* How wide a role does management envisage for its internal audit function?
2. *The quality and experience of the staff.* The more experienced the staff, generally, the fewer that are needed to carry out the task.
3. *The geography of the area.* Auditors covering a wide geographical area will spend much more time travelling and, consequently, more manpower resources will be needed to achieve the same level of coverage.
4. *The standard of systems of financial control.* Far fewer auditors are needed to look after a 'tight ship'.
5. *The rate of development.* A dynamic organisation will require more audit input into reviewing developing systems.
6. *The degree of automation/computerisation.* This can have a profound effect upon the level of input and, indeed, upon its nature.
7. *The extent to which fringe activities are carried out.* These can be handled by other review agencies (e.g. management services).
8. *The extent to which activities are centralised.* It is often easier to review a centralised function than to examine the same function carried out in a large number of outstations.

Rarely is the audit manager faced with a 'blank sheet of paper', except where a new organisation has been formed or where an audit section is to be developed where one previously did not exist. In such cases, some guidance can be obtained by referring to similar sized organisations, with the same functions, where as many as possible of the variables fall within the same range. However, in the majority of cases, an audit manager will seek to compare the size of his section with others when he considers that he has too few staff and wishes to place pressure on management to increase his manpower. By far the most effective means of doing this is through a detailed audit plan which expresses, in no uncertain terms, the risks which management are incurring by restricting the size of the audit section.

Audit staffing and structure

The staffing and structure of an audit section will, like its size, depend to a large extent on local factors. Indeed, the size of the section will itself help to determine the type of staffing and structure, as will many of the factors which influenced the size of the section. In addition to these, however, the extent to which computer systems are used, the structure and staffing of the organisation and, in particular, the finance department, and the concentration on specific aspects, such as capital expenditure or value for money, are factors to be borne in mind when organising the audit section.

Ideally, within an audit section, there should be a blend of experience, up-to-date knowledge, initiative, drive and tact. Most audit section staff are predominantly accountants, whether qualified, part-qualified or trainees. Some sections, however, favour the multi-disciplined approach, so, in addition to accountants, they employ, for example, engineers and operational research specialists. The career structure for finance staff is not generally based on the internal audit section but on the finance department as a whole. This leads to staff being transferred in and out of the audit section which can cause problems on occasions, particularly if experienced staff leave. It is important, therefore, that there is sufficient incentive, in the form of adequate remuneration and job satisfaction, for experienced staff to remain in the section.

In addition to staff engaged in traditional audit duties, there is a growing need for auditors to specialise in particular activities. Perhaps the best example of this is computer audit, although, in the larger organisations, the time is rapidly approaching when all auditors should have experience in this aspect. Other specialist areas might include contract audit and bonus schemes.

The staff of the audit section will normally be organised into audit teams, each headed by a team or group leader. The division of staff may be based on services (e.g. education in a local authority) or on functions (payroll, income, etc.) or a combination of both. Each team should be responsible for the completion of part of the audit plan and the group leaders will be involved in the compilation of this plan. Group leaders should also have some responsibility for the administration of the internal audit section as a whole, as well as for their own particular team, and should be involved in the determination of overall audit policy.

Recruitment and training

A question often asked about auditors is whether they are born or trained, to which the stock answer is *both*. There is much truth in this. Provided that an individual is reasonably intelligent, he or she should not prove too difficult to train in the technical skills of audit, but the personal qualities required cannot, in the main, be taught. Thus recruitment of audit staff can be seen on two planes. Firstly, at all levels in the organisation, the audit manager is seeking to recruit people who possess the required personal qualities. Secondly, at a senior level, he is attempting to 'buy' the acquired technical and managerial skills and experience which he would otherwise need to impart by extensive training. The training of audit staff is a costly business and one which, unfortunately, does not receive sufficient attention in many organisations. In this section, the personal qualities, for which the audit manager should be looking when he seeks to recruit audit staff, will be examined briefly before recruit training is described in detail.

Personal qualities

Auditors of long standing will be tempted to say that the only personal quality required of an auditor is perfection. It is true, however, that a higher degree of personal qualities is required of an auditor than of staff in many other disciplines. The following are the most important personal qualities:

1. *Intelligence*. If an auditor is to acquire the wide-ranging skills and techniques necessary to his profession, he must undoubtedly possess a sound intellect which needs to be balanced with a high degree of common sense.
2. *Tenacity*. Often this is quoted as the most important quality needed by an auditor and, indeed, it has a high priority, but it does need to be tempered with judgement. Too many auditors hold on tenaciously to an exhausted line of investigation.
3. *An inquiring mind*. An inquisitive nature, combined with a tendency not to accept information at face value without challenge, are vital qualities for an auditor.
4. *Imagination*. Auditors need to have an imaginative approach to their work, particularly those involved with reviews of economy, efficiency and effectiveness (i.e. value for money). Audit managers should select staff who can demonstrate a creative and innovative attitude.
5. *Good behavioural qualities*. An auditor should have the ability to get on well with his colleagues and those with whom he comes into contact through his work. Few professions test the behavioural qualities of an individual more than auditing, and much emphasis needs to be placed on this aspect when recruiting audit staff.
6. *Commitment*. The very nature of auditing work dictates that practitioners need to be largely self-motivated. Thus, whilst it is not always possible to recruit staff who regard auditing as a vocation, there should always be a discernible commitment to the objectives of audit.
7. *Good character*. It goes without saying that an auditor should have an impeccable character.

Training

It is true to say that in many professions training does not have as high a priority as it deserves and audit is no exception. At a time of recession and consequent 'cut-backs', training is often regarded as an expendable luxury. On the other hand, it is fair to say that the last decade has seen a dramatic improvement in audit skills and techniques in the public sector and much of this can be attributed to the training efforts of CIPFA, both nationally and through its regional structure. The deficiencies have tended to lie in the field of 'in-service' training.

OBJECTIVES OF TRAINING

Before the practicalities of developing a training programme are explored, it is first necessary to examine the objectives of training audit staff. Broadly speaking, the training programme should have, as its aim, the development of a wide range of audit skills, as follows:

1. *Basic technical skills*. These include flowcharting, analytical skills, use of audit programmes and internal control questionnaires, production of satisfactory working papers, and audit report writing.
2. *Professional skills*. These include a knowledge of accountancy and relevant legislation.

3. *Specialist technical skills*. These include computer audit techniques, work study and contract audit skills.
4. *Investigatory skills*. These include how to conduct a value-for-money study and how to investigate fraud and corruption.
5. *Human behavioural skills*. These include interviewing techniques, how to deal with an awkward auditee and how to persuade management to accept audit recommendations.
6. *Management and organisational skills*. These include how to conduct an audit, how to lead an audit team, and audit planning and control.
7. *Knowledge of an organisation*. This includes knowing the protocol, regulations, procedures and the decision-making processes of an organisation and knowing how it is structured.

THE TRAINING PROGRAMME

The development of a programme which will impart the various skills outlined above is no easy task and clearly not all members of staff will require the whole range of skills. A useful starting point, therefore, is to identify the skill requirements of each member of the section and thereby to assess the training needs. There are distinct advantages in involving staff in the process of identification; often their perception of their own training needs differs from that of the audit manager and may even be more accurate.

Training can conveniently be divided into four broad categories, as follows:

1. Practical experience.
2. Professional training.
3. In-service training.
4. External training.

The training programme should encompass each of these.

PRACTICAL EXPERIENCE

Often, too little regard is given to the importance of practical experience as an integral part of a training programme. The old expression that much can be learned 'sitting next to Nellie' contains a great deal of truth. Obviously getting through the work programme is of paramount importance, but, as far as is possible without interfering too much in the flow of work, staff should be given as wide an experience as possible at all levels. A surprising number of the training objectives can be met in this way.

PROFESSIONAL TRAINING

Obviously this will be restricted to those members of staff who are studying for the professional examinations of one of the major accountancy bodies. (In the public sector, the body will normally be CIPFA.) Auditing forms only a part of the syllabus and therefore such a course is designed to develop a broad appreciation of the skills and techniques needed by the professional auditor. The audit manager can expect that such a course will cover the 'basic technical skills' and 'professional skills' mentioned on page 13 and will provide a foundation to the other areas of need.

IN-SERVICE TRAINING

The in-service training programme should aim to provide a working knowledge of the organisation and to develop those other skills for which external training is not available. In-service programmes will vary considerably, therefore, and it is only possible to provide very broad guidance as to the sort of areas which might be covered. A growing trend is for 'shared' programmes, where two or more organisations join together to run such a programme. This is particularly useful where a number of adjacent small organisations find that, individually, they do not possess the necessary resources to provide in-service training.

An essential part of any in-service training programme is an induction course for new entrants which is aimed at providing the basic audit skills and a broad appreciation of the organisation. This could be centred around the CIPFA Audit Training package, which consists of a series of pre-recorded tapes and practical sessions covering the basics of audit. Delegates should emerge knowing the objectives of audit, their own part in the process and, hopefully, what to do if they identify a serious problem.

Many audit managers find it useful to designate a specific day each month for in-service training, in order that audit work can be planned accordingly, and, whilst it is not always possible to include topics which will be useful to all levels of audit staff, it is of great benefit, on occasion, to hold combined sessions which involve all levels in the organisation. Apart from creating a good team spirit, the junior members of the team will gain much from the experienced participation of the senior audit staff.

Another possible avenue of in-service training, which is particularly useful for large audit organisations with geographically-based teams which rarely meet together, is an annual conference. In this way staff can come together in a relaxed atmosphere to share problems and ideas and to participate in a programme of concentrated training.

The following are typical topics relating to an organisation which are covered by in-service training sessions:

1. Standing orders and financial regulations.
2. Accounting and budgetary control.
3. The decision-making process.
4. The direct labour organisation.
5. The organisation and management of audit.
6. Preparation for an audit.
7. Conduct of an audit.
8. Protocol and reporting lines.

The following are some more general topics covered:

1. Flowcharting.
2. Internal control questionnaires.
3. Report writing.
4. Working papers.
5. Industrial relations and the auditor.
6. Interviewing and the judges' rules.

EXTERNAL TRAINING

Many forms of external training are available and the audit manager is often bombarded with leaflets advertising courses run by professional bodies, academic institutions and, increasingly, by speculative private organisations. The public sector is also served well by an annual programme of courses run on a national basis by CIPFA and, in addition, many CIPFA regional organisations and audit groups also run extremely cost-effective courses at a local level.

External training is generally more costly than in-service training, particularly where residential courses are used, and much care needs to be taken in selecting the right courses. However, topics are covered by external courses which could never be dealt with adequately on an in-service basis in all but the largest organisations. Some typical topics are as follows:

1. Behavioural skills.
2. Computer audit.
3. Contract audit.
4. Work study and incentive bonus schemes.

In addition, it is usually possible to attract a better range of expertise (in the form of experienced lecturers and practitioners) to externally organised courses, and facilities such as video equipment are often available.

One aspect of external training which is rarely used and has many advantages is secondment. Exchanges of staff between County/Regional Councils and District Councils, Regional Health Authorities and District Health Authorities and their headquarters and regional offices, internal and external audit, and even between public and private sector organisations, all have distinct possibilities. Those few public sector organisations that have tried this have reported advantages to the individual (from the point of view of personal development) and to the organisation (from the aspect of shared techniques, procedures and ideas).

TRAINING RECORDS

Implicit in the development of a proper training programme is the maintenance of adequate training records for each member of staff. These are extremely useful in assessing further training needs and in comparing development between individuals. If an organisation has a training section, it will keep records as well as help organise the whole training programme.

Publicity

Effective auditing relies heavily upon effective communication. The importance of the more formal aspects of communication (reporting, etc.) is discussed in Chapters 5 and 6. This section deals with the less tangible, and yet equally important, aspect of communication, which can be encapsulated under the broad heading of 'publicity'. It is essential that audit managers seize every opportunity to 'wave the audit flag' in order that everyone knows that the audit section exists, is fully aware of its objectives and has complete faith in its ability to achieve these.

After every audit exercise, the audit manager will have a series of stock questions which he will ask himself, as follows:

1. Have all matters arising been dealt with?
2. Have all systems' weaknesses been rectified?
3. Are any matters to be carried forward to the next audit?
4. Has a suitable report been prepared for management?
5. Has every opportunity been taken to present the audit viewpoint to officials and board members?

On a more formal level, it is essential that the role and objectives of audit are spelt out in financial regulations, together with audit's right of access to all records and assets and the requirement for officers to account to audit and provide any explanations that are required. Such regulations are often usefully supplemented by an explanatory memorandum to chief officers which expands upon their contents.

Many audit managers find it useful to produce an 'audit brochure' which sets out the objectives of the audit section, how it fits into the organisation and what its lines of reporting are. Excellent examples of brochures are freely available in the public sector. These often provide a useful 'calling card' when visiting a new location or when dealing with a new officer.

Magazine articles and various publications which promote the audit image are a useful means of publicity. These can be suitably emphasised (modern fluorescent pens are ideal for this) and given to the chief executive or director of finance, or left in a strategic place in the members' library or rest room. However, care should be taken not to overpublicise as this can do more harm than good.

CHAPTER 4

Audit planning and control

In common with other labour intensive services, audit is an expensive resource and it follows that those charged with the responsibility of managing that resource should plan carefully how it is to be used and should monitor actual performance against that plan. This fact has been well recognised and, in recent years, the subject of audit planning and control has featured time after time in the lecture programmes of local audit groups and in papers presented at seminars and conferences. The arguments are therefore well rehearsed; nevertheless they are sufficiently important to merit reproduction here. Certainly any publication which aims to cover comprehensively the subject of audit in the public sector would be incomplete without some advice on planning and control.

The planning cycle

To be effective, the planning and control of any function must follow a cycle, and audit planning and control is no exception to this rule. Figure 1 illustrates the various and distinct stages in the cycle. First we must plan our audit work and then we must conduct the audits along planned lines. However, the cycle is incomplete and, indeed, the planning process is rendered less effective if we then fail to monitor our success in achieving planned objectives and, in the light of this, review the plan in order to begin the cycle again. In this chapter each stage of the planning cycle will be examined in depth.

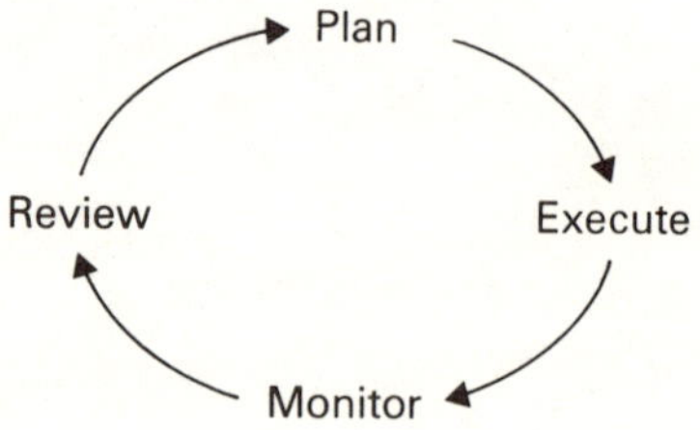

Fig. 1 *The planning cycle.*

Preparing a plan

Audit planning divides conveniently into three broad levels, as follows:

1. Strategic planning.
2. Tactical planning.
3. Operational planning.

Strategic planning

Strategic planning is by far the most important. This is an exercise in determining the broad objectives of the audit function and how those objectives will be achieved. In theory, little or no heed should be given, at this stage in the process, to the available manpower resources, but in practice some regard must be given to this if the strategic plan is to remain an achievable exercise. The following is a list of some of the more important questions which should be answered in the formulation of the strategic plan:

1. What are the objectives of the audit function?
2. How should the audit section be structured to achieve those objectives? Should there be audit teams? Should work be allocated on a subjective basis (e.g. payroll, creditors and contracts), an objective basis (i.e. services) or a geographical basis?
3. Are any areas of activity to be omitted from the audit review?
4. What is the minimum acceptable level of audit coverage?
5. Are specialist staff to be employed (e.g. computer auditors)?
6. Where are the auditors to be based (i.e. centrally or in divisional offices)?
7. Is the audit approach to be system or regularity based?
8. To what extent will the work of audit be co-ordinated with that of other review agencies? (For example, management services, work study, and O & M.)
9. Does the auditor have any responsibility for the review of management information systems?
10. Are any resources to be earmarked for value-for-money projects?

It is vital that the strategic plan is seen as a flexible and dynamic policy document which must change to meet the ever-developing needs of the organisation. For this reason, it is not possible, or even desirable, to recommend any duration for a strategic plan. It must be constantly amended to take account of changing circumstances.

Tactical planning

A tactical plan, on the the other hand, ought to cover a defined period, and 12 months seems to be the most popular timescale. Again, flexibility must be the keyword and the audit manager should not regard the tactical plan as a sacrosanct expression of immutable audit policy. Put simply, the tactical plan assesses the workload imposed by the strategic plan and attempts to reconcile this with the resources available to carry out that work. It is, therefore, an exercise in balancing an equation – the *resources/workload* equation.

The first stage in balancing the equation is to determine the manpower resources that are available. This relatively simple task involves an assessment of the total man-days from which should be deducted the estimated days required to cover holidays, sickness, training and vacancies. It is important, for reasons which will become obvious later, that no allowance is made at this stage for any allocation of staff to 'non-audit' duties. Thus the resources side of the equation will take the following form:

Total man-days available		=	
Less	Annual leave Bank holidays Other leave (e.g. flexi-leave)	=	
Less	Estimated sickness	=	
Less	Estimated vacancies	=	
Net resources available			man-days

The second stage of the process is to assess the workload. This is by far the most complex side of the equation and entails a comprehensive review of all of the activities of the organisation. Having regard to the strategic plan, and the decisions taken therein, the audit manager must express each area of audit activity in the form of a man-day target. In doing so he should not look at the available resources at this stage, but should consider the targets to be an expression of his professional opinion as to the resources required to achieve the required level of audit coverage as stated in the strategic plan. In arriving at each target, the audit manager will have in mind a number of factors, as follows:

1. The resources required to conduct the audit in the past.
2. Any history of unusual difficulties, such as frauds and irregularities.
3. The strength of the financial systems operating in the area and the extent to which he will be able to rely upon them.

Many audit managers advocate the use of extensive risk indices to allocate resources to individual audit tasks. These usually involve the calculation of aggregate income and expenditure figures, weighted by various risk factors, which are then used pro rata to determine the allocation of the available man-days. However, it is often the case that, at the end of such laborious calculations, the audit manager will examine the result, and if it does not match his professional assessment of the needs of the audit task, he will adjust the weightings until it does. For this reason, such an approach is not recommended. Nevertheless, the assessment of risk does constitute an important part of the audit planning process and, at this stage in the development of the tactical plan, it is recommended that the audit manager should allocate a simple risk assessment to each audit task. Let us assume, for example, that the audit manager has decided to use a three-level risk index – high, average or low. He should consider each audit task and, with regard to his knowledge of the organisation and the varying risks associated with different kinds of income expenditure and assets, he should allocate one of the three risk factors to each task.

Frequency of audit plays an important part in the formulation of the tactical plan, and again the recommended approach is for the audit manager to allocate to each audit task the ideal frequency which his professional experience tells him is necessary. It should then be possible to calculate the annual man-day effect of each audit task and thereby the workload in terms of total man-days per annum. Thus the workload calculation will take the following form:

Audit task	*Risk factor*	*Man-day requirement*	*Frequency*	*Annual effect*
a	High	20	½ yearly	40
b	High	60	3 yearly	20
c	Average	10	Annually	10
d	Low	50	5 yearly	10
e	Average	10	Monthly	120
f	High	25	Annually	25
etc.	etc.	etc.	etc.	etc.
			Total man-day requirement	x

The two sides of the equation can now be compared. The possibility that the resources will exceed the workload is so remote as not to be worth considering here, and it is almost inevitable that the audit manager will be faced with reducing the workload somehow, in order to balance it with the available resources. There are three basic choices open to the audit manager, as follows:

1. He can omit certain tasks from the programme of work, possibly those designated as low risk.
2. He can reduce the man-day allocation to individual audit tasks and thus carry out the audits in less depth.
3. He can extend the frequency of the audits.

The likely outcome will be a combination of all three but, as a matter of principle, the third choice is favoured. Even low risk tasks, if they are left completely out of the programme, will eventually become high risks, and if the man-day allocation is reduced and only superficial reviews carried out, the whole audit process will be devalued. By far the best method of reducing the workload is to extend the frequencies of the 'low risk' tasks until they are regarded as 'average risk' and then, if necessary, to extend the frequencies of selected 'average risk' tasks until they become 'high risks'. In this way the tactical plan can be balanced.

APPROVAL OF THE PLAN

We now reach a crucial stage in the planning process and one which is, surprisingly, often omitted by audit managers – the approval of the plan. It is a comparatively painless exercise for management to agree a strategic plan with the audit manager, as it involves decisions about audit policy without reference to available resources. It is not quite so painless, but, none the less essential, for management to consider the tactical plan. Bear in mind that the tactical plan, as well as being a schedule of audit tasks to be completed, is also an expression of the risks which management is taking in providing fewer audit resources than are necessary to achieve the agreed strategy at the depth and frequency which the audit manager considers appropriate. Therefore it is important that the tactical plan receives approval at that level of management which has the power to allocate, or at least to recommend the allocation of, additional manpower resources should it consider the risks to be too high. It is equally important that the tactical plan should draw attention to those tasks which have had to be omitted and to the areas where input has been restricted or where frequencies have been extended in order to balance the equation.

Once the tactical plan is agreed upon, we can move to the final part of the 'plan' section of the planning cycle – the production of an operational plan.

Operational planning

In simple terms, the operational plan divides the tactical plan into manageable bites of usually not more than a few weeks' duration. In deciding which tasks to include in the operational plan, the audit manager will have regard to a number of factors, including the following:

1. *Timing*. The planned frequency of the task, and the elapsed time since it was last completed, must be considered.
2. *Geographical location*. It is often desirable and, indeed, more economical to undertake a number of audit tasks together in the same geographical vicinity.
3. *Availability of special expertise*. Some tasks may require an input from specialist staff and the availability of such staff will thus influence the operational plan.
4. *Special events*. It is sometimes advantageous to coincide audit visits with special events, such as payday, the month or year end, or at a time when income or expenditure is at its peak.
5. *Seasonal factors*. Many activities are seasonal and this may well have a bearing upon the timing of an audit task; for example, there would be little use in conducting an audit of a grasscutting bonus scheme in the middle of winter.
6. *Work patterns*. There will be times when the auditor will be less welcome than usual because of workload peaks. Reviews of the budget preparation system, therefore, should not be scheduled at a time when the accountants are busy preparing estimates.
7. *Information received*. A 'tip-off', anonymous or otherwise, may well influence the audit manager to bring forward a particular audit task.

These are some of the more common factors and there will, no doubt, be many more.

Once the operational plan has been fixed, the audit manager will communicate its contents to his staff in the form of work instructions. Arrangements will vary between organisations, but such instructions should always be in writing and should state, *inter alia*, the nature of the task, the staff to be involved, the time allocated to the task and details of the work to be carried out. It is likely that the written instructions to staff will include a detailed audit programme. (Audit programmes are dealt with in more detail in Chapter 5.)

The audit manager may separate value-for-money activities and systems review from the transaction-based activities, in which case individual value-for-money and systems review tasks will have been included in the tactical plan. Alternatively, each audit task may contain an element of systems and value-for-money reviews.

Whatever the detailed instructions contain, if the planning process is to be successful it will be necessary for the audit manager to employ an effective 'cut off'. In other words, he must be able, by various means, to maintain the schedule of audit tasks within the allotted time. However, if it becomes necessary to conclude an audit task before the scheduled work has been completed, it is essential that it is the less important aspects of the work which are omitted. A useful technique to ensure that this is achieved is to allocate a priority rating to each individual activity. Each activity is then completed in order of priority, thus leaving the least essential tasks to the end. In this way the important matters will be dealt with at each audit and, by rotating the less important tasks, they, too, will receive attention on a reasonably regular basis.

Many audit managers build into their tactical plans an element to cover contingencies, such as unplanned work (special investigations, frauds, etc.), and to extend target times when this is thought necessary. In this way, a more flexible approach to 'cut off' can be adopted. Others regard an in-built contingency as a resigned acceptance that the planned targets will never be achieved. To fail to recognise that unplanned work will arise and/or targets will have to be exceeded occasionally is unrealistic. Therefore, to omit a contingency element from the tactical plan is equally unrealistic.

Executing the plan

The physical process of conducting audit tasks in accordance with operational plans is described in detail in other chapters and leads in logical sequence to the monitoring stage.

Monitoring

The objective of the monitoring stage is to assess the degree to which the plan has been achieved in practice, in terms of both quality and quantity. Quality is obviously a subjective issue and is dealt with in more detail in Chapter 10. In this section the quantity aspect will be dealt with, in other words, the process which assesses the degree to which the planned targets have been achieved. Many systems are used by audit managers, most of which revolve around the completion of time sheets by audit staff to indicate how their time has been spent. It would not be appropriate to reproduce these systems in detail here but, in order to exemplify the monitoring process, one relatively simple system, which has been found to work well in practice, will be described, as follows:

1. A record card is maintained for each audit task. It shows the nature of the task, planned frequency, risk factor and the time target.
2. Time sheets are kept by audit staff, recording how their time has been allocated between audit tasks to the nearest quarter day.
3. Record cards are issued to audit teams, and targets may not be exceeded without the permission of the audit manager.
4. Using the time sheets and record cards, team leaders produce a monthly summary of staff time showing time spent on:
   (a) Designated tasks.
   (b) Work in excess of planned targets (contingency).

(*c*) Unplanned exercises (contingency).
(*d*) Training.
(*e*) Holidays.
(*f*) Sickness.
(*g*) Vacancies.

5. The audit manager maintains a chart which indicates, in graphical form, the planned cumulative target for each element of the plan. Monthly summaries are then plotted against the cumulative targets, thus providing a broad picture of performance (see Fig. 2).

Fig. 2 *A chart showing the planned cumulative targets for each element of the audit plan.*

Reviewing the plan

The final stage in the process is to use the information gained from the monitoring stage to review the success of the plan. This will be done informally after each operational plan and more formally before the production of a new tactical and/or strategic plan. In this way, successive audit plans will be built upon experience and thus should be increasingly successful.

The objective is to compare actual time spent on various sections of the audit with that which was planned. Where the plan was clearly generous, it can be reduced accordingly and, where it proved to be inadequate, a decision can be taken as to whether the allocation should be increased for future periods or whether the programme of tests in that area should be modified to reduce the input. However, the review should not be restricted to a mathematical exercise. The opportunity should be taken at each review to re-examine the objectives of the audit and to consider whether the correct strategy is being used – in other words, to review the strategic and tactical plans.

The benefits of audit planning (and some of its pitfalls)

One of the most common criticisms of auditors is that they have no deadlines to achieve, and thus are left to complete tasks in their own time. Payclerks must prepare payrolls by payday, creditors sections must pay invoices by the date due, debtors sections must despatch bills on time and accountants have budget and 'closing down' cycles to achieve. An audit plan imposes similar constraints and demonstrates that auditors, too, have targets to achieve.

As already mentioned, audit is regarded, in many organisations, as an available pool of labour for emergencies. It is often an easy option for management to divert audit resources to undertake work in other sections of the organisation to meet such emergencies. It becomes less easy if the audit manager is able to refer to an audit plan and to express such diversions in terms of lost audits, the consequences of which must be accepted by management.

Auditors tend to have areas of work which they particularly favour and other areas which they dislike. An audit plan prevents such bias reflecting itself in the allocation of audit time (unless, of course, the audit manager himself is biased!).

Perhaps the most important benefit arising from the audit planning process is that it imposes the discipline of reviewing the whole spectrum of audit work, assessing the risks and priorities involved, and determining the adequacy of the available audit resources. However, there are pitfalls in the audit planning process which the wise audit manager will attempt to avoid. Audit plans can become too complicated and cumbersome so that far too much time is spent on completing detailed time sheets and records and too little time is spent on actually carrying out the audit tasks. Inflexibility can be a problem and the audit plan can become regarded as an end in itself. Perhaps the most common pitfall of all is to break the planning cycle; the most likely break point is after the 'execute' stage. To fail to complete the full cycle is to risk losing many of the inherent benefits of the process and, in particular, to fail to gain from the evolutionary process of audit planning.

Developments in audit planning

As the techniques of audit planning have evolved, greater use has been made of the computer, particularly in larger organisations which maintain extensive audit sections. Many of the quantitative elements of the plan can be computerised successfully, thus reducing the amount of time needed to maintain time records. As the real cost of computing continues to fall, this becomes increasingly an option open to audit managers.

Not all audit plans are expressed in man-days. Many use cost as the controlling factor and such an approach is particularly common in the field of external audit. A man-day approach takes no account of the vast difference between the value (and cost) of a qualified senior and an unqualified junior assistant, unless some form of man-day weighting is used. A costed approach, where targets are expressed in financial terms, is thus more realistic and in many ways more meaningful. The simple process of assessing the full cost of a man-day, including overheads, at various audit grades can, on its own, have a dramatic effect on audit managers and audit staff alike. Few of us are aware of precisely how much an hour or a day of our time costs our employers, and such knowledge can have a major impact upon the way we use our time. There is no doubt that decisions involving the allocation of audit time become more meaningful when expressed in financial terms. For example the question 'Can I have an extra 20 man-days to complete this audit?' becomes, say, 'Can I spend an extra £1,400 on this audit?' Similarly, a decision to devote 400 man-days to the audit of works contracts becomes a decision to spend, say, £28,000 on the process.

CHAPTER 5

Audit documentation

In most disciplines, good documentation is almost as important as good practical work. In the field of audit, documentation assumes an even greater degree of importance. The most thorough of audits, if not supported by detailed, accurate and comprehensible documentation, is of little practical value. The very nature of audit work, often involving the criticism of the work of others, attracts challenge. To counteract this, the auditor must record his work and his findings in such a manner as to provide evidential support for his recommendations. In this chapter, the various aspects of audit documentation are examined in detail and ways of recording audit work in such a manner as to maximise its impact are described.

Audit programmes

It seemed at one time that every audit examination paper contained at least one question which started with the phrase 'compile an audit programme to cover the examination of . . . '. With the trend towards a systems-based approach to audit, involving less emphasis on regularity audit, such questions have become less prevalent. This suggests that audit programmes have assumed a less important role in the armoury of the auditor. Nothing could be further from the truth, particularly in internal audit. Audit programmes remain an important and extremely useful means of communicating instructions to audit staff, and provide an excellent basis for recording work done.

At its simplest, an audit programme is a list of audit activities to be carried out. In effect, it is a further stage of detail from the operational plan. If the operational plan can be said to be an expression of the audit tasks to be completed over a period of days/weeks/months, then audit programmes record the detailed tests and checks to be undertaken in order to complete each task. In other words, they comprise a series of written instructions from the audit manager to his staff, recorded in such a way as to constitute a programme of work to complete a particular audit task.

Opinion varies as to whether audit programmes should be extremely detailed, where they identify every single activity required of the auditor, or whether they should provide only broad guidance as to the areas to be covered. In the authors' view, much depends upon the experience of the audit staff involved. Relatively new or inexperienced staff will need a detailed audit programme to tell them precisely which tests and checks they are to carry out and the extent to which each test is to be conducted. On the other hand, more experienced staff only need broad guidance and, indeed, a detailed audit programme might generate an 'automatic' approach, thus stifling initiative.

The merits of internal control questionnaires (ICQs) will be discussed later in this chapter, but it must be said that these are simply another form of audit programme aimed at listing the various stages to be followed in reviewing a particular system of internal control. For convenience, each stage is written in the form of a question; nevertheless, ICQs are audit programmes.

Many publications already exist which provide examples of audit programmes to cover every conceivable aspect of audit work. It is not the intention to duplicate these here; however, in order to illustrate audit programmes and to exemplify the extremes of detail which can be involved, several examples of audit programmes have been included in Appendix 2.

Many audit managers adopt the practice of cross-referencing audit programmes to systems records so that auditors can readily see how the compliance tests which they are conducting fit into the overall pattern of procedures. As the systems records will identify the weak points in internal control, this will also assist the auditor to concentrate his efforts on the tests covering these areas.

In Chapter 4, the use of priority ratings as a means of effecting a 'cut off' to the audit, whilst ensuring that the more important tasks are always carried out, was described. The audit programme is a useful vehicle for expressing those priorities. Each item in the programme can be allocated a priority rating and those with a high priority may then be tackled first. In this way the audit can, if necessary, be concluded at an early stage, leaving only the low priority items uncompleted.

Working papers

If there is one single area that attracts more justifiable criticism of the auditor than any other, it is the standard of working papers. Clearly this should not be so. Audit working papers are the prime documents upon which the eventual audit criticisms and recommendations will be based, and it follows that they should be of the highest order.

Working papers comprise a record of all the work done during an audit, and show the tests and checks undertaken and the extent to which these have been completed. In conjunction with the systems records and audit programmes, with which they should be cross-referenced, they build a comprehensive picture of the completed audit task. Various types of audit working papers are in use and commonly these will include the following:

1. *Standard working papers*. These are cross-referenced, where appropriate, to the audit report and other working documents.
2. *Query sheets*. These are lists of questions which arise during the audit, together with answers received. These should be cross-referenced to the standard working papers.

3. *Lists of unsettled items*. These are carried forward to the next audit, and are cross-referenced to the original standard working papers.
4. *Audit summary sheets*. These are often used by team leaders to summarise the main items arising from the audit.
5. *An audit programme*. This will often form a working paper itself, in as far as it may be used to record the extent of tests and checks undertaken.

It is an important facet of supervision that audit staff should be required to initial every working paper which they complete. Similarly, senior staff charged with reviewing the work should also be required to initial working papers, as this encourages a responsible attitude and enforces a supervisory discipline which might otherwise be lacking.

Many audit managers find it useful to devise standardised working papers as this assists them to locate easily the various component parts of the audit as they conduct their reviews. However, it is far more important to ensure that working papers meet certain criteria, as follows:

1. Each working paper should be properly titled with the name of the audit, the date and the nature of the work recorded.
2. The audit file reference should be recorded, together with any cross-references to the audit programme, systems records and any associated working papers.
3. All working papers should be neat, legible and prepared with the same degree of care and attention as the audit report itself.

Perhaps the most effective test of the adequacy of a working paper is that, if it fell out of the audit file and was picked up by an informed stranger, he should be able to determine what it is, what it records, who had produced and checked it and in which file it belongs. How many working papers would pass such a test?

Audit files

Well-kept audit files are a sign of an efficient and well-managed audit section. An important part of preparing for an audit involves reviewing the previous year's audit, and this can be rendered difficult, if not impossible, by poor audit files. This is particularly so if the auditor is unfamiliar with the audit. In these circumstances, he will need to place great reliance upon the existing audit files. Similarly, the audit report is built on the foundation of its supportive working papers and it is vital that these are filed in a manner which facilitates ease of information retrieval.

Audit files can be conveniently divided into two categories – *permanent information files* and *current files*. Permanent information files contain data which are needed at each audit. Examples are as follows:

1. Systems records and internal control questionnaires.
2. Staffing structure.
3. Standing orders and financial regulations.
4. Accounting and other relevant instructions.
5. Audit programmes.
6. Salary, wages and bonus rates.

Current files, on the other hand, contain all of the working papers and reports relating to the current audit, including completed audit programmes and ICQs.

Permanent information files must be kept up to date and it is an important role of the audit manager to make sure that his audit staff are kept supplied with the most up-to-date permanent information possible.

It is impossible to generalise about the content of current audit files, but, as a guide, they might contain the following:

1. Audit working papers cross-referenced to query sheets, 'next audit notes' and the audit report.
2. Audit query sheets cross-referenced to the audit report.
3. The completed audit programme, showing the work done and who did it, cross-referenced back to working papers and query sheets.
4. Completed systems' ICQs and other working papers.
5. The audit summary report cross-referenced to all of the above documents.
6. The final audit report, together with a copy of the supporting letter to management.
7. A record of management decisions and proposals arising from audit recommendations, indicating the date for implementation.
8. A list of matters carried forward to the next audit – 'next audit notes'.

It is important that auditors remember that audit files are high security records and that they often contain confidential, and even controversial, information. Too often audit files are left unattended on desks at the audit location or are stored at headquarters in an insecure manner. 'On location' they should be under the supervision of senior audit staff at all times; in the audit office they should be locked in secure cabinets and only made available to authorised personnel.

Audit reports

The purpose of an audit report is to convey to the recipient the results of the audit and the problems and weaknesses that have been identified. Its objective is to persuade management to take remedial action. It is, in fact, the 'shop window' for the considerable and expensive audit work which has gone before. Much excellent audit work can be wasted if the resulting audit reports are unprofessional and ineffective.

Where, in the midst of an audit, a serious problem is discovered which requires immediate attention, it may be necessary to issue an interim report; however, audit reports are normally produced at the end of the audit process. Generally speaking, at the end of an audit one of three situations will apply, as follows:

1. There may be no matters to be raised.
2. There may be only a few minor matters to be raised.
3. There may be major criticisms or so many minor matters as to constitute a major problem.

Where there are no matters to be raised, the external auditor will have his certificate to fall back on as a natural conclusion to the audit. The internal auditor, however, is faced with the alternative of issuing a report (or a letter) which says he has found nothing amiss, or of doing nothing and effectively leaving the audit in mid-air. Many opt for the latter course, preferring not to write a positive or even congratulatory letter for fear that time may prove them wrong. In so doing they miss a golden opportunity to create good working relationships, to dispel the view that auditors only criticise and, more importantly, to applaud and encourage good internal control. At the same time, the line manager, who has suffered the inconvenience of the audit presence in his office, is left wondering whether or not the audit has been concluded and whether the wrath of the chief executive is about to fall upon him. Without doubt, the audit manager should have the courage of his convictions and issue a 'clean bill of health' report where this is justified.

Where only a few minor criticisms emerge at the end of the audit, it is essential that these are not elevated to a position of over-importance by the manner in which they are reported. The report should be congratulatory and should simply make passing reference to a few minor issues which require attention and which are relegated to an appendix. In this way, the minor matters will receive attention, but the auditor's perspective and sense of proportion will be seen to be sound.

Finally, where major criticisms occur, or so many minor items are raised as to constitute a major problem overall, it will be necessary to prepare a 'full blown' audit report, and the remainder of this section will deal with the production of that report.

The independence of the auditor dictates that he should have the right to report in his own name and without censorship on any aspect of the organisation. To justify this, he must be able to produce a high quality professional report and he must have clear reporting lines. There should be no restrictions placed upon him as to whom he may report and he must have the recipient of the report clearly in mind at all times whilst he is preparing it. The report must be written in such a way that the recipient will easily understand it; the objective is to communicate rather than to impress.

The report should be as concise as possible, as, the briefer it is, the more impact it is likely to have because busy line managers will take the trouble to read it. It is always useful to summarise the main points contained in the report at the beginning, in order that senior management can assimilate the key issues quickly.

Jargon should be avoided at all costs, as should vague terms, such as 'a few', 'many' and 'a sample'. It is of little use to tell a line manager that a sample of transactions has been tested and a few have been found to be wrong. He needs to know how many have been tested, how many are wrong and in what way they are incorrect.

Finally, it is recommended that a 'due date for implementation' of agreed recommendations is incorporated in the report. In this way, management is more likely to take prompt action and the auditor will have a useful yardstick against which to measure management's response to his proposals.

Systems records

Most modern audit sections have adopted a systems-based approach to their audits in the belief that this represents a far more efficient and effective use of scarce and expensive audit resources. The systems-approach encompasses the concept that prevention is better than cure. In such circumstances, the systems records maintained by audit assume prime importance. The techniques of systems audits will be discussed later, when the various records which are associated with the approach will be dealt with.

Systems records are 'permanent information' documents which, not surprisingly, form a record of the major systems of internal control. The purpose is to help the auditor to understand the systems fully, to assist him to identify weaknesses and key control features and to provide a permanent record upon which subsequent systems audits may be based.

Three methods of recording systems are commonly in use – the narrative format, the flowchart format and the combined format. The narrative format involves committing the system to paper in the form of the written word. It has the advantage of being simple and requires little formal training. It is easily understood by the layman and it is relatively easy for a new auditor to come to grips with the system quickly. However, each individual has a unique style of expression which lends itself readily to misunderstanding and it is comparatively easy to 'gloss over' complications in a system using the narrative style.

Flowcharts, on the other hand, require a certain level of acquired skill which involves training. They are not easily understood by the uninitiated and it can often take a long time to comprehend a system fully. However, they are rarely ambiguous and they have the considerable advantage of imposing the discipline of tracing every single aspect of a system to its ultimate conclusion. It is not possible to 'gloss over' complications in a flowchart without making a deliberately false record.

Many flowchart formats are available, perhaps the most popular in the public sector is the modified version of the 'Skinner and Anderson' format recommended by CIPFA. Perhaps the most successful method of recording systems involves a combination of both narrative and flowchart styles. The flow of documents is recorded in the normal flowchart manner, but key operations are cross-referenced to a narrative description which provides a far more flexible and descriptive style.

The identification of weaknesses, and the amendments to systems agreed subsequently with management to obviate these, will be recorded in the normal audit report and resulting correspondence, as will the subsequent checks to test compliance of the amendments with the existing system. It is important to stress that systems records, to be of benefit, must be kept completely up to date. Hence it is vital that audit is notified immediately of any changes to the systems so that the records can be amended and the system reassessed.

A common method of testing existing and previously recorded systems is by means of purpose-designed internal control questionnaires. These consist of lists of questions expressed in a way such that a 'yes' answer is acceptable and a 'no' answer constitutes a weakness that requires attention. The questions are designed to probe key areas of internal control and are intended to assist the auditor to review internal controls. However, an auditor does not rely solely upon the answers given to an ICQ as his means of reviewing internal controls. ICQs need to be supplemented by compliance tests to ensure that theory and practice accord with each other. (Appendix 3 provides some examples of ICQs.)

Sources of information

It is important that management makes sure that the people for whom it has responsibility have the resources which they need to carry out their designated tasks. One of the main resources needed by an auditor is information; without this he cannot function properly. It follows, therefore, that one of the fundamental duties of an audit manager is to ensure that his staff have as much information as is possible at their disposal. This does not mean, of course, that the audit section should have a library of similar proportions to the British Museum. It simply means that auditors should be made aware of the information that is available and where it can be obtained. It is not necessary, for example, for the section to keep copies of every statute, but auditors should be kept informed of those which are relevant to their duties and where they may be seen.

The information required by auditors can conveniently be divided into three broad categories, as follows:

1. *Permanent information*. This information is needed at all audits.
2. *Temporary information*. This information is needed only at one particular audit.
3. *Operational information*. This is information which is obtained in the course of the audit.

The responsibility for obtaining operational information obviously rests with the auditor himself, and the audit manager's role lies in ensuring that permanent and temporary information sources are comprehensive and up to date.

Permanent information

Permanent information will include the following items:

1. Statutes.
2. Statutory instruments.
3. Circulars (government and other).
4. Guidance from CIPFA and other professional bodies.
5. Comparative statistics from various sources.
6. Technical reference books.
7. Professional magazines and publications.
8. Standing orders, financial regulations, accounting manuals and various memoranda of accounting instructions.
9. The minutes of the organisation.
10. A chart showing staffing structures with positions and grades.
11. A list of establishments and locations.

12. A list of officers authorised to place orders, together with any limitations (e.g. 'food only' or 'goods/services below £1,000').
13. A list of officers authorised to certify invoices for payment, together with any constraints.
14. Descriptions in either narrative or flowchart form of all major systems of internal control.

Temporary information

The following are some examples of temporary information:

1. Recent officer reports to members/the board.
2. A current staff list.
3. A list of present pay points.
4. A current price list and approved charges.
5. Recent computer exception reports.
6. Relevant newspaper cuttings.

Operational information

It is not possible to produce a comprehensive list of examples of operational information because of the wide range of such information that is required by an audit section. Suffice it to say that this information is directly linked to the specific requirements of individual audits. This will include samples of various transactions (e.g. invoices, orders, inventory items and payments to employees over 65) which will be used in the course of the audit.

CHAPTER 6

Conducting an audit

So far little has been said about the practicalities of internal audit. Before any real audit work can be undertaken it is necessary to set objectives, determine management procedures and set down the ground rules for documenting the audit. These aspects have been discussed at length in the preceding chapters and in this chapter the practical issues of conducting an audit will be discussed. These include the necessary preparatory work, the practical aspects of conducting systems and regularity audits, and the reporting lines and the range of options which are, or at least should be, open to the audit manager.

Preparation for an audit

Too often audit staff arrive at an audit location unprepared for the task. This results in a waste of the auditor's and the auditee's time and it is damaging to the efficient image of audit. However good the relationship between the auditor and the auditee may be, there is bound to be some resentment over the time the auditee has to spend in providing information and explanations. If this time can be kept to a minimum, and if the auditor has done a fair amount of advance preparation, then much will have been done to maintain good working relationships.

Advance notice

An important question to be answered at the preparation stage is whether advance notice of audit should be given to the auditee. Much depends upon the nature of the audit; for example, it would not be appropriate to give advance notice of a spot check on cash holdings or of a visit to investigate a suspected fraud. Generally, however, advance notice should be given. It would be totally unfair to expect an auditee, without advance warning, to rearrange his schedule in order to accommodate an audit visit. If, however, notice is given the auditor can make sure that all records are available and that every member of staff who is needed is present. This can avoid much wasted time on both sides. Too much notice should not be given, however, as this would allow incomplete records to be brought up to date and errors and omissions to be rectified. A happy medium would be one to two days' notice.

Previous audits

Much can be gained from reading the previous audit files – items brought forward for action at this visit and areas of past difficulty can be noted, a 'feel' of the audit can be gained, and a general picture can be built up of the efficiency of the organisation to be audited.

Audit programmes

The audit programmes to be completed should be obtained and studied. Any additional work to be done should be agreed upon and priorities should be established in order that the most important tasks are completed first. Thus, if the audit has to be concluded before all items have been covered, at least the major matters will have been dealt with. It should be stressed that the high priority items may include checks which, in isolation, may not appear to be important but, because they have been omitted for a number of audits, they have assumed a higher level of priority.

Systems

From the systems records the auditor should familiarise himself with the major systems of financial control. Certainly these records will be available at the audit location, but there is nothing more annoying to an auditee than an auditor who continually has to stop to consult his records, thus demonstrating his lack of knowledge and preparation.

Personnel

This may seem a fairly simple point, but it is surprising how many auditors arrive at the audit location not knowing the names of the officer in charge and the senior staff with whom they must deal. A good auditor will also have found out about the personalities of the key members of staff and even their hobbies and interests. In this way a useful 'ice-breaking' conversation can be readily initiated.

Protocol

Allied to the need to know the names of key personnel is the need to observe protocol and this may well vary from department to department. Many chief officers have quite strong views about who should be consulted at the beginning and end of an audit and throughout its course. In the absence of any stated rules of protocol, it is suggested, as a general principle, that no work should be done in a department without the chief officer (or his nominee) being informed beforehand and, at the commencement of a visit to an outstation (for example, a transport depot or children's home), the auditor should first report to the person in charge. Similarly, it is courteous to report again at the end of an audit visit, if for no other reason, to thank the person in charge for his co-operation and to discuss with him the more important matters that have arisen.

Preselection of data

Much work needs to be done in advance of the audit in preselecting various items of information which will be used. Examples of paid invoices may be selected for checking against goods received, stores or inventory records, or for a physical verification of work completed. Lists of controlled stationery issued to the establishment may need to be prepared for eventual verification at the audit. Special audit computer interrogations may need to be run to provide details of various matters, such as numbers and grades of employees, overtime paid, analysis of expenditure over individual creditors, outstanding debtors over three months old, etc.

Selection of staff

The right blend of audit personnel needs to be achieved. Regard should be given to the complexity and importance of the audit, the volume of work to be completed and any special operations required. The audit manager should also consider the personality of the auditee, and thus the behavioural qualities needed by the auditor. In this way a balanced team can be organised which will be best suited to the task in hand.

Systems audit

As mentioned in Chapter 5, the modern trend in audit is towards a systems-based approach. This is not to say that the regularity audit is unnecessary – and, indeed, the next part of this chapter is devoted to this – but that prevention is better than cure. Thus the establishment of secure and efficient systems of control is of paramount importance.

It is necessary to recognise, however, that the establishment of such systems is management's task, not internal audit's. Often audit is seen as the 'systems design team'. The danger here is that it would be particularly difficult for audit to adopt a totally independent position if it were required to review a system which it had designed itself. In addition, it is unlikely that management would adopt with any enthusiasm a system which had been imposed upon them. Such a system would always be regarded as 'audit's system' and the tendency would be to allow it to flounder or even to sabotage it.

There are certain distinct stages in a systems audit and the remainder of this section will discuss the practical implications of these in the following order:

1. Identifying the major financial systems.
2. Recording the systems.
3. Testing the systems.
4. Reviewing the controls and identifying the weaknesses.
5. Eliciting improvements.
6. Compliance testing and reviewing.

There is one golden rule that every auditor should bear in mind when reviewing systems – no control should cost more than the likely loss if that control did not exist. In other words, in recommending improvements in systems, the auditor should have regard to the economy of controls. It is too often the case that auditors try to produce the 'perfect system' by means of elaborate and costly procedures which simply cannot be justified.

Identifying the major financial systems

There can be no hard and fast rules on this. What is a major financial system in one organisation may not be so in another. However, in general terms, a major financial system will control a significant part of the income, expenditure or asset holdings of the organisation. These generally will include the following:

1. Payroll systems.
2. The payment of creditors.
3. Debtors.
4. A cash income system.
5. Postal remittance systems.
6. Stocks and stores systems.
7. Inventory systems.
8. A terrier of property.
9. Loans and borrowing.
10. Investments.
11. Cash security.
12. Bank reconciliation.
13. Controlled stationery.
14. Petty cash expenditure.
15. Procedure for preparation of budget.
16. Budgetary control.
17. Project appraisal.
18. Control of manpower.
19. Capital expenditure controls.
20. Pension benefits.

Recording the systems

As already discussed, systems records can be in either narrative or flowchart form (or possibly a combination of both). Narrative format has the advantage of being easy to understand but it is too easy to gloss over complications. The completion of a flowchart imposes the discipline of following every stage of the system to its absolute conclusion. To a trained eye, a flowchart is more readily understood and a particular activity can quickly be traced through the system. Many flowchart formats are available and they all achieve much the same objective – to provide a visual record of the system in operation.

Testing the systems

At this stage the systems will probably have been recorded on the basis of a verbal description provided by management. Unfortunately, the tendency is to describe the systems as they should operate, rather than how they actually operate in practice. It is only human nature to cut corners, but often this will obviate controls which have been built into systems. To overcome this, it is necessary, having recorded the systems, to select a sample of transactions and to 'walk them through' the systems. In this way any departures can be identified and recorded. Thus an accurate picture can be obtained of how the systems work in practice.

Reviewing the controls and identifying the weaknesses

The next stage in the exercise is to review the controls, i.e. to find out whether internal check and other control factors exist. It is also important to identify any weaknesses in controls in the form of an absence of internal check and other control factors. At the same time, it may be possible to locate inefficient or unnecessary procedures.

Eliciting improvements

Where control weakness and inefficient or unnecessary procedures have been identified, these should be drawn to management's attention and recommended improvements should be requested. Management can be guided as to the sort of improvements which are necessary, but the audit section should not be seen to be redesigning the whole system. The possibility exists, of course, that management may refuse to make any changes to the system, claiming that it is fine as it is. There are various methods of dealing with situations such as this. One thing that an auditor can do is to write to the line manager, recording his criticisms and stating that he (the line manager) has the ultimate responsibility and will, no doubt, be prepared to be totally accountable for any problems which might arise from the weaknesses which have been identified in his systems. This approach usually has the desired effect.

Compliance testing and reviewing

It is necessary, at regular intervals, to test compliance with the agreed system, particularly with the key control features. Internal control questionnaires specially designed for the system are a useful means of achieving this. It is also important, from time to time, to review the system in the light of changing circumstances to make sure that the controls continue to be relevant and up to date.

Regularity audit

Regularity audit is that part of the audit which tests, by means of sampling transactions, that the 'rules' of the organisation have been adhered to, that material fraud and significant levels of error are not in evidence and that the organisation is acting within its statutory powers.

In practice it is impossible to divorce the systems audit from regularity audit and, indeed, for that matter, from value-for-money reviews. They are all part of the same process. However, in the interests of simplicity, each part is dealt with separately – value for money is covered in Chapter 9.

The extent of the regularity audit will be influenced significantly by the results of the systems audit. Thus, in an area where systems are strong and are adhered to in practice, the regularity audit can be reduced. Conversely, where procedures are weak and little confidence can be placed in controls, then a more extensive regularity audit will be necessary.

Regularity audit is usually organised on the basis of audit programmes which do the following:

1. They test the various rules, both internal and external, that have been set up to see that the activities of the organisation have complied with them, and that, consequently, the income and expenditure of the organisation have been handled properly, the assets have been kept secure and the various financial transactions have been recorded properly. These rules will include standing orders, financial regulations, accounting manuals and instructions, inventory regulations, stock control procedures, etc.
2. They test that no significant levels of error occur.
3. They test that there are no significant frauds and other irregularities.
4. They test that there are no *ultra vires* transactions and thus that the activities of the organisation fall within its statutory powers.

Regularity audit is regarded by many as the bread and butter of an auditor's work and it does in many respects represent the layman's view of the role of the auditor. However, it is important to ensure that this somewhat mundane image of regularity audit does not lead to a robotic approach. Regularity audit requires flair and imagination if it is to achieve anything.

The art of sampling pervades most aspects of audit work, but perhaps none more so than regularity audit. Sampling, statistical or otherwise, is a wide-ranging subject about which many books have been written, so it is not the intention to deal with it here in any detail. Opinions vary amongst auditors as to the benefits of sampling. Some auditors regard scientific sampling as being of little value, whilst others advocate a comprehensive statistical approach to the selection of audit samples and the interpretation of their results.

Statistical sampling is particularly useful in error-testing large volumes of transactions. Using various statistical tests one can determine, to high levels of confidence, the likely degree of error, whilst checking relatively few transactions. Many auditors find random number tables a useful means of selecting samples. Stratified sampling enables the auditor to form an opinion about various sizes of transaction; for example, the selection and checking of samples of contracts from various value bands can help to evaluate the degree of control existing in those bands. This may, for example, lead to the conclusion that there is less control on contracts below £10,000 and, indeed, more losses occurring at that level. Without stratified sampling, the auditor would inevitably concentrate more of his time on high value contracts.

The biased approach to sampling – the selection of the obvious error/irregularity – is more pragmatic. Providing that one is not seeking to form an opinion about a large volume of transactions, this approach does serve wonderfully to focus audit attention on areas where it is most likely to be productive and, indeed, where it is likely to have the greatest impact in terms of results and publicity.

For all its unglamorous image, regularity audit can produce dramatic results. Many managers have been persuaded to improve systems controls, not because of a major review of the system, but because imaginative regularity tests have proved that the control weaknesses have actually resulted in errors or irregularities of material proportions.

Reporting lines

The independence of the audit manager and the importance of his freedom to report in an unrestricted fashion to any level in the organisation, upon any topic, have already been discussed. Here, these concepts will be expanded upon and reporting lines in general will be covered.

Reporting lines can be either formal or informal and it is important to stress that it is the authors' view that formal reporting lines should be established at the start, committed to writing and communicated to all relevant levels in the organisation. This can do so much to avoid misunderstandings and disagreements.

It should be established to whom the audit manager reports in an administrative sense and, in a local authority, this will usually be the director of finance. Different arrangements exist in many other public sector organisations, with audit managers reporting to, for example, the management board. What is essential is that this reporting line in no way detracts from the auditor's independence and under no circumstances inhibits his freedom to report. A prime example of an administrative reporting line which would be inhibitive is an audit manager who reports to an assistant director of finance who also has responsibilities for certain line functions. It would be an extremely virtuous assistant director who did not attempt to use his position in such circumstances to modify an adverse audit report on one of his own areas of line responsibility.

It needs also to be established to whom an audit manager reports in a professional sense on the following items:

1. Planning and progress.
2. General issues of financial control.
3. The results of specific audit exercises.
4. Fraud, corruption or other discovered irregularities.
5. Issues of value for money.

Reports on planning and progress will normally be submitted to the officer to whom the audit manager is administratively responsible; in local authorities normally the director of finance. Similarly, with reports on general financial control which give a general picture of various departments, it can be of immense value if a report on these topics (perhaps in summary form) is also submitted to the chief executive. It is perhaps with the chief executive that an informal reporting line can also be of most value.

The results of particular audit exercises should generally be destined for the officer who will have to put right any problems or weaknesses. This may well range from a 'middle manager' to a 'chief officer', depending upon the nature of the report and the seriousness of the weaknesses. A useful arrangement which works well in practice is for such reports always to go to the middle manager (e.g. head teacher, matron, works manager, etc.) with a copy to the chief officer (e.g. director of education, director of social services, director of central services, etc.). This arrangement should apply whether the report contains criticisms or merely records that all is well. The practice of informing the chief officer only when something is wrong is not to be encouraged. It is as useful for a chief officer to know which of his sections/establishments are running well, as to know which are causing problems. However, where a report is seriously critical of the middle manager, it would be wise to direct this only to the chief officer so that he may take positive remedial action. Audit reports should always state the names of all persons to whom they have been sent.

A separate arrangement should exist for reports on frauds and irregularities and, again, it is important that this is formalised and fully understood by everyone. Line managers should be required to report immediately to the audit manager whenever any irregularity is suspected. The person to whom the audit manager reports at the conclusion of his investigation will vary considerably. Generally, an audit manager will be expected to submit his report on a serious irregularity to the following:

1. The officer to whom he reports administratively, say, the director of finance.
2. The chief executive.
3. The chief officer concerned.

Some audit managers will report directly to the police without consultation and others will be constrained by elaborate reporting and consultation processes.

Reporting lines on value-for-money reports are relatively easy to establish. Clearly, the prime responsibility for value for money lies with line management. It follows, therefore, that any recommendations to improve value for money should be channelled to the chief officer in charge of the service concerned. To encourage positive thought and, even more important, positive action, it is often useful to provide a copy for the chief executive.

One area fraught with difficulties involves reporting lines to local authority members. Opinions range from the 'tell them nothing' stance to the view that members should be kept fully informed of internal audit activity. Advocates of the former policy claim that it would inevitably lead to a 'member' takeover of internal audit management and direction, leading to the use of audit as a political weapon. Those in favour of keeping members informed claim that such a policy would add strength to the audit process. As is so often the case, it is a matter of individual judgement as to the likely effect. Certainly it is not suggested that all detailed audit reports should be channelled to members, but there can be distinct advantages in submitting regular progress reports, general reports upon standards of financial control and specific value-for-money reports at quarterly intervals or half-yearly or annually.

CHAPTER 7
Specialist areas

An auditor in the public sector will be expected to have a knowledge of how to approach the audit of specialist areas, which include the following:

1. Computer audit.
2. Contract audit.
3. Audit of incentive bonus schemes.
4. Audit of investments.

Each area is a subject in its own right, but, in a general publication of this nature, it would not be appropriate to discuss these in depth and, indeed, each one could merit a publication of its own. However, this chapter sets out, in a concise manner, the salient points to be covered during an audit, for the guidance of auditors in the public sector.

Computer audit

The overall objectives of computer audit can be defined under the following five headings:

1. Systems procedural control.
2. Systems development control.
3. Administrative and organisational control.
4. Procurement or enhancement of computing facilities.
5. Use of resources.

The principles of computer audit are not different from those applying to all other spheres of audit. However, because of the technical aspects of computers and their associated systems, the controls in operation and the effectiveness of those controls are not as easily ascertained and tested as those of manual systems. A recommended audit approach to assessing the adequacy and adherence to the controls and procedures in the area of computer audit is set out in a statement issued by CIPFA. This is a very concise and succinct summary of that situation and is well worth quoting in full. The CIPFA statement reproduced below identifies the various aspects for review by audit.

CIPFA statement on computer audit

The Institute commends the following statement to local and public authorities in considering the auditor's role in relation to computers.

Introduction

The Institute Council considers that computer audit principles are no different from those which operate in all other spheres of audit. It is the application of those principles which differs. Owing to the technical qualities of computers and their associated systems, the controls in operation are not as easily ascertained, nor is the effectiveness of these controls as easily tested. Management will need to ensure, therefore, that it has sufficient technical support under its direction to cope with the audit of computers.

Audit objectives

Although the audit approach to computers will vary, the overall objectives of computer audit can be defined under five headings, as follows:

1. *Systems procedural control.* Review of systems to ascertain whether they incorporate adequate procedural controls and that these controls are not invalidated by any subsequent amendment to the system.
2. *Systems development control.* Review of procedures in operation to ensure that the development and maintenance of systems within the organisation result in well documented computer systems incorporating adequate controls and meeting properly defined user requirements.
3. *Administrative and organisational control.* Review of the adequacy of controls to promote secure and efficient day-to-day operation of the installation.
4. *Procurement or enhancement of computing facilities.* Review of the procedures for proposing and approving the procurement and enhancement of computer facilities and the accuracy and completeness of the information which is provided to assist management in coming to a decision.
5. *Use of resources.* Review of the procedures by which management exercises control over the use of computing resources.

Attainment of computer audit objectives

To attain these objectives, it will be necessary for the auditor to be concerned with all stages of the computing process. In seeking to test the adequacy of controls and procedures within computerised systems, the auditor should consider, too, how best use may be made of the computer to assist him in his audit so as to maximise the effective use of audit resources.

Consideration of all the areas to be examined, together with a discussion on the application and management of computer audit, is contained within the Institute's publication, *Computer Audit Guidelines*. The primary areas for audit examination within each of the five overall objectives as defined above and in that publication are summarised below.

1. **Systems procedural control**

The auditor should review the following:

(a) *Input controls.* The procedures adopted to control input to the system to ensure that as far as is reasonably possible, it is genuine, complete, not previously processed, accurate and timely.

(b) *Processing controls.* The processing controls within the computer system to ensure that the correct data and program files are used, that all data is processed, accounted for and written to the appropriate file, and that data conforms to predetermined standards or falls within specified parameter values.

(c) *Output controls.* The output controls to ensure that all expected output is produced, that it is complete and appears reasonable and is distributed on time and in such a way that confidentiality is maintained as necessary. Adequate controls should be maintained to ensure that errors and exceptions are properly investigated and resubmission of data made where appropriate.

(d) *Audit trail.* The maintenance of a complete audit trail to ensure that an item can be traced from input through to its final resting place, and a final result can be broken into its constituent parts.

2. **Systems development control**

The auditor should review the following:

(a) *Project management.* The formal mechanism, process or system by which proposals for developing (or substantially amending) systems are considered in the light of the available resources of the organisation.

(b) *Project approval.* The project approval procedures which must be in accordance with those procedures governing the preparation of a feasibility study which sets out the costs and benefits of computerising the project, together with the nomination of a project control team responsible for the project.

(c) *System and program specifications.* System and program specifications which should be prepared after due consultation with all interested parties and with the user's approval to the project before further work continues.

(d) *System testing and implementation.* The design, preparation and implementation of the system testing which must conform to agreed procedures including participation at the testing stage of the user.

(e) *Training of user.* The establishment of a training programme for all members of the user and computer departments who will be involved in the implementation and operation of the system.

(f) *Amendment.* The procedure for maintaining the system and supporting software, which should be of a standard at least as high as that of the initial development of the system.

(g) *Documentation.* The maintenance of system and program documentation throughout all stages in the design, development and operation of the project.

3. **Administrative and organisational control**

The auditor should review the adequacy of the following:

(a) *Organisational control.* Organisational controls, which deal with the organisation of the responsibilities of all involved in the computer process and the standards established for their efficient working.

(b) *Operational control.* Operational controls, which relate to all aspects of the data preparation, data control and operating functions.

(c) *File and software control.* File and software controls which govern the access to and protection of all magnetic files and to the data contained on them both by way of software controls and physical controls.

(d) *Terminal control.* Terminal controls, which govern the access to and processing performed by all terminals connected to the computer installation.

(e) *Environmental control.* Environmental controls, which deal with the risks of fire, flood, vandalism, sabotage and theft and the adequacy of insurance cover.

4. **Procurement or enhancement of computing facilities**

The auditor should review the adequacy of the procedures relating to the following:

(a) *Establishing the need.* The establishment of the need for the hardware and software.
(b) *Feasibility study.* The preparation and presentation of a feasibility study containing a recommendation and calling for a decision.
(c) *Specifying requirements.* The implementation of that decision by specifying precisely the requirements for the hardware or software.
(d) *Appraisal and decision making.* The appraisal of the prospective suppliers' products and a decision on which to adopt.
(e) *Installation.* The installation of the product and its hand-over to the customer after adequate testing.
(f) *Post-implementation review.* The conduct of a post-implementation review to determine whether the benefits claimed have been realised within the costs specified.

5. **Use of resources**

The auditor should review the adequacy of the procedures by which management exercises control over the following:

(a) *Costs.* Identifying the costs of computing.
(b) *Staff.* Identifying how best use is made of staff resources.
(c) *Hardware.* Evaluating how effective and efficient use is made of computing facilities.
(d) *Software.* Evaluating how effective and efficient control is exercised over the development and use of software.
(e) *Data.* Identifying the availability, accuracy, relevance and completeness of data used and produced by computing facilities.

Contract audit

Public authorities spend vast sums of money each year on capital expenditure. The process is long and complex, commencing with the formulation of a project and concluding with the final account and post-contract review. In the past, and even today in some organisations, the auditor has been deeply involved in the final account stage. However, whilst this stage is important, so are the others, and it is vital that the auditor is involved in reviewing and testing systems throughout the whole capital project process.

CIPFA has produced a statement on contract audit which summarises, in a concise manner, the areas which should be examined by audit. This was first produced in response to the section on contract auditing in the former Chief Inspector of Audit's report for the year ended 31 March 1979. It is reproduced here in full.

CIPFA statement on contract audit

The Institute Council has considered the section of the chief inspector of audit's report for the year ended 31 March 1979 on contract auditing (paragraphs 108–120). It is the Council's view that all chief financial officers should review their organisation's approach to this aspect of audit work. It is felt that it is timely to emphasise the relevance of the Institute's publication, *Financial Examination and Audit of Capital Contracts*, to the development of a modern professional approach to contract auditing and, in order to assist in this task, the Council offers the following guidelines.

Audit objectives

Although the audit approach to building and engineering contracts in organisations will vary, the overall audit objectives should be universal and should include the following:

1. Assessing and reporting on the adequacy of the organisation's standing orders relating to the contracts and associated financial regulations.
2. Reviewing and reporting on the extent to which procedures comply with the policies and procedural rules of the organisation.
3. Reviewing the adequacy of systems for controlling the operation of contract works from the initial planning stage to post-completion assessment.
4. Reviewing and reporting on the extent to which management information is prompt, adequate, accurate and designed for the needs of all the users.
5. Appraisal of the system for controlling and recording the utilisation of resources, including staff.
6. Reviewing the use of consultants and agency services provided by other organisations.
7. Monitoring the arrangements for the security of the organisation's assets and for recovering the cost of rechargeable works.
8. Prevention and detection of fraud, error and impropriety.
9. Identification of losses due to waste, inefficiency, etc., and recovery where appropriate.

(*Financial Examination and Audit of Capital Contracts,* Part I, Chapter 2.)

Methods to be used in attaining these objectives

To attain the objectives stated above it will be necessary for the auditor to be concerned with all stages of capital works, and the check list given below, whilst not necessarily exhaustive, gives some indication of the areas which should be included in the audit plan for examination.

1. **Pre-contract stage**

(a) The system for and effectiveness of project appraisal within the organisation.
(b) The systems for admitting contractors to the approved list (where one is maintained) and for reviewing their performance and current viability.
(c) The methods for the selection of contractors invited to tender.
(d) The system for regulating the tendering procedures and the letting of contracts.
(e) The system for reviewing the suitability of conditions of contract and tender documents.
(f) Insurance, liquidated damages and bonding procedures.

2. **Currency of contract**

(a) The system and documentation for providing financial information to enable costs to be adequately controlled, including reporting procedures.
(b) The system of on-site control regulating valuations of work for interim payments.
(c) The system for the examination and control of price fluctuations.
(d) The system for the control and issue of variations.
(e) The system for the receipt and evaluation of contractual claims.

In order to satisfy himself on the above matters it will be necessary for the auditor to visit site/divisional offices.

3. **Post-contract stage**

(a) The system for ensuring that, when the final account is produced, it is complete and accurate.

(*b*) The system to ensure that liquidated damages have been recovered where appropriate.
(*c*) The system for post-contract reporting.
(*d*) The system for post-completion assessment.

4. **Other matters**

(*a*) The system for the examination and evaluation of any request for an *ex-gratia* payment.
(*b*) The system for dealing with liquidation and bankruptcy.

The Institute Council wishes to draw attention to the provisions of the Local Government Act 1972 and the Accounts and Audit Regulations 1974 which define the duties and responsibilities of the responsible financial officer and, in particular, to the provisions regarding internal audit. Quite clearly, the arithmetical check of the final account advocated by the Manpower Commission in 1952 can no longer be accepted, and the requirement to maintain a current internal audit of the accounts of the body must clearly be extended to contract accounts. The current contract audit approach is endorsed by the chief inspector of audit in his report.

Training

The Institute Council recognises that there is a need to provide adequate training for contract auditors, with particular reference to current contract auditing. The Institute proposes, therefore, to promote courses at national and regional level.

Relationship with other professions

The Institute Council recognises that there is a need to ensure that all professions engaged in contract work have a clear appreciation of the respective roles their members play at all stages of the contract. The Council therefore welcomes the fact that the contract audit working party is in the process of developing statements (with the Royal Institution of Chartered Surveyors and other professional bodies) on the roles of the technical officer and the internal auditor. When finalised and approved by the appropriate institutes, these should go some way to ensuring that misunderstandings regarding their relationship in the field of capital account auditing need not arise.

Standing orders and financial regulations

The Institute Council recognises that there is a need to ensure that standing orders and financial regulations relating to contract procedures are clear and contain all the necessary safeguards relating to financial control. The Department of the Environment is currently revising model standing orders, and when these are published, the contract audit working party intends to compare them with the model produced by CIPFA in 1973 and make such recommendations to the Council as seem necessary.

Audit of incentive bonus schemes

For the purposes of this chapter, an incentive bonus scheme is defined as being any arrangement whereby an employee receives an additional payment in return for an increase in productivity. Such schemes proliferate in the public sector and it would be useful to outline some of the types of scheme commonly found.

Types of incentive bonus schemes

Nomenclature varies from organisation to organisation and the terms used in this book are those commonly in use, as follows:

1. *Productivity agreement.* A scheme whereby a fixed productivity payment is made in return for a pre-agreed increase in productivity, e.g. when a vehicle mechanic resigns, the remaining mechanics in the garage could agree to undertake the existing workload without a replacement, in return for an apportionment of part or the whole of the cost of the employee who had resigned.
2. *Historical target scheme.* Individual operations are allocated time targets based upon the time the tasks normally (i.e. historically) take to complete. Bonus payments are based upon performance against those targets. Schemes such as these are often found in direct labour organisations.
3. *Fixed task scheme.* An individual or a group of individuals is allocated a fixed task to complete in the day or week (e.g. a refuse collection round) and this is calculated to take up the working day/week at a predetermined level of performance. The fixed payment (inclusive of bonus) is made upon completion of the task, irrespective of the time taken.
4. *Measured day-work schemes.* These are similar to fixed-task schemes, except that the task is not so readily defined. The workload is measured over a long period and a level of performance is assessed in order to reflect the average effort required of the workforce to complete all aspects of the work over a given period. A bonus payment is incorporated into the wage payment and this will continue to be paid as long as the workload is completed. Such schemes lend themselves to work which has seasonal variations, such as horticultural work. The work of a parks department gardening gang will vary from week to week and month to month depending upon the season, but, year upon year, it will remain much the same.
5. *Variable-task schemes.* Perhaps the most common form of scheme, these relate to groups whose tasks vary considerably but where individual operations repeat themselves frequently. For example, a garage mechanic may well carry out many different tasks during the day but, over a period of time, each task will crop up again and again (e.g. replace Ford Transit clutch). Using work study principles, a value is attributed to individual tasks which is expressed in 'standard minutes'. Depending upon total standard minutes earned over a period, an individual's performance is calculated and an appropriate rate of bonus paid.
6. *Multi-factor schemes.* Productivity may not be the only factor which management wishes to encourage. Other criteria, such as quality, time-keeping, attitude, appearance, etc., may be important. A multi-factor scheme allows an element of the bonus payment to reflect each criterion, which means, for example, when work of poor quality is produced, the element of the bonus payment relating to quality is lost.
7. *Consolidated schemes.* It is argued that, when employees work under incentive conditions for a long period, they become conditioned to achieve

a certain level of output. Thus, if the productivity-linked incentive is removed, productivity will not fall. A consolidated scheme aims to pay a consolidated wage, including an element to cover average past bonus earnings, thus saving the costly overhead of productivity measurement.

Objectives of audit

Broadly speaking, the auditor should set out to satisfy himself that the bonus scheme is providing value for money, so that, for every pound spent on bonus, additional productivity of at least an equivalent value is received. In order to examine the objectives of a bonus scheme in more detail, these will be subdivided into objectives relating to the management of a scheme and operational objectives. The degree to which the auditor will concentrate upon one aspect or the other will depend largely upon his assessment of the first line supervision controlling the scheme, and of the ability of management. When both are considered good, it should be possible to limit involvement on the operational aspects. Where this is not the case, then considerably more effort will be needed on operational aspects.

In order to achieve the objectives relating to the management of schemes, an auditor will wish to satisfy himself that the following criteria are fulfilled:

1. Schemes should be soundly based and viable.
2. Schemes should be kept up to date in the light of changing circumstances and practices.
3. Schemes should be operated in accordance with agreed specifications.
4. Management and supervision should be able to control the schemes effectively.
5. Work should be efficiently organised in order that productivity is not lost through employees waiting for instructions or resources.
6. The monitoring systems should be capable of presenting management with a realistic picture of the success, or otherwise, of the schemes.
7. Targets or values should be reasonable and correctly applied in practice.
8. Schemes should achieve the objectives which they set out to achieve.

Operationally speaking, the auditor's objectives will be the following:

1. To ensure that employees are not claiming to have carried out work which they have not done, and that the system of control is such that any attempts so to do would be brought to light.
2. To ensure that there has been no attempt to 'hold over' work from one period to another.
3. To ensure that increased productivity has not led to reduced quality.

The CIPFA 'role and objectives' statement emphasises the need for the auditor to establish good working relationships with others. Nowhere will these relationships be more severely tested than in the field of auditing incentive bonus schemes. There is every chance that an auditor's recommendations will have some influence on the earnings of the workforce and this can lead to a strained relationship with the employees, and with their trade unions. This, in turn, could lead to industrial unrest, with a consequent effect upon the work programme and a resulting deterioration in relationships with line management and supervision. In addition to all of this will be the ever present problem of professional indignation generated by challenging work study decisions. All in all, this is a very difficult area which requires the utmost tact and diplomacy, coupled with balanced judgement.

It is not possible to identify every conceivable problem that an auditor may encounter in reviewing bonus schemes. It is intended, therefore, to concentrate upon the more commonly occurring problems and to suggest various courses of action which an auditor might take. In the interests of clarity, this section has been divided into two broad areas – the examination of new schemes and the examination of ongoing schemes.

The examination of new schemes

It is often the case that the first indication that the audit manager has of a new scheme is when he is given a scheme specification which has been fully agreed at all levels and is due to be implemented in a short space of time. It is difficult, if not impossible, to implement any material changes at that stage without causing immense problems. In this case, the auditor may have some post-implementation criticisms of the scheme, with the benefits of hindsight. If the auditor involves himself at the design stage he could have some impact on the scheme; however, this suggests that the auditor should become a part of the system. The auditor has to choose whether he helps to shape the new schemes at the design stage or whether he accepts them as they are.

Assuming that the auditor decides to involve himself in a pre-implementation review, then his three main objectives should be the following:

1. To ensure that the scheme is soundly based on proper work study principles and is viable.
2. To determine that the report to the committee which will authorise the scheme contains a proper financial appraisal, indicating the financial benefits and setting off against these all the likely scheme costs.
3. To establish that a proper monitoring system has been developed which is capable of keeping management apprised of the success (or otherwise) of the scheme.

In attempting to achieve the above objectives, the auditor will focus his attention *inter alia* upon several prime areas. Obviously this is not an exhaustive list and each scheme will suggest unique areas of investigation.

SCHEME OBJECTIVES

Undoubtedly the scheme will have been set up with certain aims and objectives and it is important at the outset to establish what these are. The scheme may have been designed to do the following:

1. To reduce costs (for example, by reducing overtime or staff numbers).
2. To provide an improved service.

3. To absorb work currently being carried out by contractors (for example, deprivatisation).
4. To clear an accumulation of work.
5. To meet a combination of the above objectives.

If the auditor is unaware of the objectives of the scheme, it will not be possible for him to assess whether those objectives are likely to be met.

REFERENCE PERIOD

It is vital that the auditor should examine the scheme reference period (i.e. the period which work study has used as the basis of producing the scheme and assessing its potential benefits). It must be of a sufficiently lengthy period to cover the full cycle of work; obviously this will vary according to the nature of the work. This period must be taken at a truly representative time and thus avoid distortions caused by peaks and troughs and any other unusual factors. It should be remembered that the reference period forms the basis for the whole financial justification for the scheme and, if it is not truly representative of the workload, then the data presented to the policy-making body may well be inaccurate and misleading.

VALUES

The auditor should examine the methods adopted in arriving at values in order to do the following:

1. To satisfy himself that a sufficient number of measures has been used to obviate distortion.
2. To satisfy himself that normal work methods have been employed during the study period.
3. To satisfy himself that, wherever possible, original values have been devised and the use of borrowed or synthetic values has been minimised.

INTERNAL CHECK

It is vital to ensure that the proposed supervision and authorisation systems include a proper separation of duties between the person responsible for authorising the bonus claim and those who benefit from the scheme. It is often the case that first line supervision benefits directly from the scheme, thus providing an incentive to inflate group bonus earnings.

INCENTIVES

Some incentive schemes do not really provide an incentive. The auditor should make sure that a particular scheme will, in reality, relate payment to performance in such a way as to provide a proper incentive.

MONITORING SYSTEMS

Monitoring systems must provide management with an accurate picture of the operational success, or otherwise, of the scheme, in order that prompt and effective remedial action can be taken. It follows, therefore, that audit should ensure that the proposed monitoring scheme is likely to be able to achieve this.

FINANCIAL BASIS

Perhaps the most important 'pre-scheme' activity for the auditor is to ensure that the financial justification presented to the policy-makers is accurate and comprehensive. The auditor must be sure that the financial benefits of the assessed scheme are realistic and that, deducted from these, are all the costs which are associated with the scheme. These should include the following:

1. The cost of the bonus payment.
2. The cost of calculation by bonus clerks and by computer.
3. The cost of scheme design and maintenance, including monitoring.
4. The cost of any additional supervision.
5. Related pay rises to support staff and supervision.

The examination of ongoing schemes

Inevitably, with a systems-based approach, the auditor will spend a good deal of time upon the systems operated by management to control the schemes. These will range from the overall programme of scheme reviews, which will be discussed later in this chapter, through the individual scheme control systems to the first line supervision arrangements.

MANAGEMENT CONTROL SYSTEMS

It is extremely important that each scheme is supported by an effective management information system which provides meaningful data in a form which management can readily understand and which is sufficiently sensitive to highlight significant deviations from expected results. It is also important that management takes positive corrective action whenever this is necessary.

The control of manpower input is important, particularly in the case of productivity schemes and fixed-task schemes where the workload is pre-determined to equate to a specific performance level at an agreed level of manpower. If the manpower input is allowed to increase without control – for example, by means of additional overtime – then the required performance level would not be achieved and the bonus payment could not be justified.

It is also vital to establish, for fixed-task schemes and particularly for the more broadly based productivity agreements, that the workload or task is being completed. It is easy to concentrate upon inputs and to forget the output in terms of quantity and quality.

In the case of work study-based variable-task schemes, performance levels provide a useful barometer for management, and hence for the auditor. Consistently high performances could, of course, indicate an extremely hard-working individual or group. However, they could also indicate an increase in output compensated by a reduction in quality, incorrect work claims, wrong or misapplied values/targets or any number of other unacceptable reasons. Similarly, consistently low performances, other than in the initial stages of a scheme, could mean that the scheme is simply not succeeding in providing an incentive to increase output. Fluctuations in performance from a non-bonus earning situation to a bonus-earning position, if regularly repeated, could indicate the carrying forward ('holding over') of work unclaimed in one work period to be claimed incorrectly in the following work period, thus deflating performance in the former period and inflating it in the latter. In this way an individual who finds it difficult to achieve bonus-earning performances could fraudulently receive bonus in alternate work periods.

The system of first line supervision is extremely important to the proper control of a bonus scheme. Ideally a supervision system should contain an element of 'pre-inspection' to ensure that work is not inflated beyond the level that is necessary. In some cases, the nature of the work is such that post-inspection is impossible and pre-inspection thus assumes even greater importance.

The specification of a satisfactory level of random work inspection is important, and these levels must be adhered to in practice. The best supervision systems involve the recording, by first line supervision, of the work it inspects, and a follow-up examination, by management, of a proportion of that work and other unchecked work.

OPERATIONAL CHECKS

Operational areas upon which the auditor will wish to concentrate his efforts will include work methods, measurement methods, the allocation of allowances and synthetic values, and levels of lost time and unmeasured work.

Changes in methods of work which are not taken into account in amendments to task values can result in the payment of unearned bonus. For example, if a manual task is mechanised, it will almost certainly be completed more rapidly and with less effort. This should be reflected in a reduction in the value or target associated with that task.

Inaccurate methods of measurement can often lead to a considerable inflation of performance levels. It is often the case, for example, that areas of land are measured by pacing them, rather than by accurate measurement. Experience suggests that this can lead to errors as large as 40 per cent.

The claiming of various allowances is a common area of abuse. Allowance claims for such activities as travel between jobs are often exaggerated and it is common for allowances to be claimed for activities which have not been completed. For example, many bonus schemes involve a daily or weekly vehicle cleaning allowance. A brief examination of the vehicles will reveal whether this is regularly carried out.

The use of synthetic values (i.e. the use of a value or group of values relating to a similar task when no value exists for the operation which has been completed) should be treated with caution. It is often the case that factors have been built into the 'synthetic' value which are totally inappropriate to the task undertaken.

Careful regard should be given to levels of lost time and, where possible, ways of verifying the accuracy of claims should be found. For example, claims for wet days can be compared to newspaper weather reports.

Unmeasured work is perhaps the single most common area of difficulty for the auditor. It is usual for the first six hours of unmeasured work to attract no bonus but, thereafter, to be paid at the average performance returned on measured work. Thus there is a temptation to book difficult jobs to unmeasured work and thus obtain an overstated performance. The auditor should check that only 'one-off' jobs and those which are outside the scope of the scheme, or have an extremely variable work content, are included. All other tasks should be measured and targets set for bonus purposes.

CONSOLIDATED SCHEMES

A number of organisations are leaning towards consolidated bonus schemes because of the attractions of fixed payments. In this way, complicated calculations are avoided and a reduction in work documentation is effected, thus saving in administration. The theory, as stated earlier, is that where staff have become accustomed to working under direct incentive conditions for a length of time, when the direct incentive is removed, provided that their overall income is not reduced, they will continue to work at the incentive performance levels. Hence the time which has previously been spent on booking work which has been completed and calculating bonuses will be released for more productive purposes.

The theory of continuing high performances does not necessarily work in practice, thus consolidated schemes need to be supported by even stronger management information systems which monitor the continuation of previous levels of output, both in terms of quality and quantity. The auditor will need to satisfy himself to ensure that positive action is taken by management whenever the monitoring system reveals deficiencies.

SCHEME REVIEWS

Pressure on management from a variety of sources will sometimes result in rather hurried, and sometimes over-generous, reviews of schemes. Conversely, some schemes can become totally out of date, and thus out of line with reality, through the lack of a proper review. It follows, therefore, that the auditor needs to establish that a proper programme of scheme reviews has been established with acceptable review frequencies and, equally important, that it is adhered to in practice.

As far as individual reviews are concerned, the auditor should treat these as though completely new schemes had been devised and should apply to them all the audit tests which he would apply to new schemes.

Audit of investments

In the public sector, investments of any substance generally relate to pension and superannuation funds. There are, of course, other minor investment areas, such as trust funds, but these are usually of little significance and, in any case, the same audit principles apply as with pension fund investments.

As far as local authorities are concerned, in England and Wales it is the County Councils, and in Scotland the Regional Councils, which operate superannuation funds on behalf of all other local authorities in their area. In addition, there are other non-local authority admitted bodies that participate in the fund and the auditor will need to establish the full extent of participating bodies.

Organisations faced with the responsibility for managing pension and superannuation fund investments have two broad alternatives, as follows:

1. *Internal fund management.* This is the internal employment of investment experts in order to convert the broad Policy decisions of the 'investment panel of trustees' into practical investments.
2. *External fund management.* This is investment expertise which is 'bought in' from the private sector. By far the majority of organisations opt for this latter alternative.

Obviously the form of fund management will have some bearing upon the nature of the audit, since the auditor of an internally-managed fund will need to pay much more attention to investment systems controls than will the auditor of an externally-managed fund.

The audit of investments can conveniently be broken down into six broad areas, as follows:

1. Examination of the system of control.
2. Transaction testing.
3. Compliance with statutory provisions.
4. Verification of assets.
5. Temporary use of surplus cash.
6. Performance of the fund.

Each aspect will be examined in some detail.

Examination of the system of control

The organisation should produce a comprehensive code of practice and conduct for its investments staff and this is particularly important where the fund is managed internally. This should set out, in unequivocal terms, the degree of independence which is required for investment staff. The code should prevent investment staff from benefiting personally from privileged information or from directing funds in such a manner as to benefit themselves or their kin.

The systems of control over the purchase and sale of investments, the collection of dividends and interest, the payment of brokers' commission, and the receipt of entitlement in respect of bonus shares and rights issues should all be examined for weaknesses. Attention should also be given to the physical control of deeds, property titles and share certificates.

The employment of consultants and advisers is an area in which the auditor should be interested. Fees vary considerably and the auditor should satisfy himself that the organisation has obtained good value from the fee and that no one firm is favoured unfairly against another.

Transaction testing

Each system of control should be transaction tested to ensure compliance with established procedures; any breaches should be drawn immediately to the attention of management.

Compliance with statutory provisions

The statutory provisions are set out in the Trustee Investments Act 1961 (as amended) and the degree to which a fund may invest in various aspects of the market is strictly controlled. The auditor should make sure that the investment portfolio of the organisation does not exceed the sector limitations.

Verification of assets

If at all possible, the auditor should try to verify all assets at the same time. Registered stocks and shares, together with bonds and debentures, should be checked against the actual scrip certificates. An approach on a sample basis should also be made to the registrar, in order to make sure that the certificates produced relate to investments currently held in the name of the fund and to verify the validity of inscribed stocks and shares. Certificates should also be obtained in respect of National Savings Bank and Trustee Savings Bank deposits, Post Office issues and various charity investments. Deeds should be seen in respect of mortgages, and loans on deposit and certificates of title should be produced for all direct property investments.

Temporary use of surplus cash

The daily balance of cash should be closely monitored and the auditor should satisfy himself that this is being properly calculated and invested temporarily at the best possible terms.

Performance of the fund

This is by far the most difficult aspect of the auditor's role in relation to investments. However, it is vital that the auditor satisfies himself as to the performance of the fund, as compared with other funds, and with the investment market in general, in respect of both capital growth and revenue return.

Because the investment of funds is to some extent speculative, it is not appropriate for the auditor to have regard to the specific performance of individual investments, unless these are so large as to have a significant overall effect on the performance of the fund. Inevitably there will be some investments which are not very successful and others which prove to be highly beneficial. It is the overall effect of the portfolio which is important and it may well prove useful for the auditor to examine the performance of individual groups or sectors of investment.

The overall objective should be to ensure that the information placed before those charged with determining investment policy is accurate and comprehensive, and that the policies are in the best interests of the contributors to the fund, whether they are individuals or participating bodies.

CHAPTER 8
Fraud and corruption

It is more than likely that an auditor in the public sector will be required to investigate a fraud at some stage. A fraud investigation requires specialised knowledge and techniques, and needs to be handled with extreme care. Any mismanagement of a potential fraud could have far-reaching consequences. Very little has been published on the subject of fraud and corruption and, other than attendance at courses and seminars, there are only limited opportunities for auditors to gain experience and become proficient in this type of investigation. In fact, most experience is gained from an actual fraud investigation.

This chapter is intended to be a guide to auditors in the public sector and is based largely on the authors' experiences of actual fraud and corruption investigations. It provides a review of the auditor's responsibility in fraud investigation, and includes attitudes towards fraud, fraud statistics, types of fraud, the issues to be considered during a fraud investigation, including referral to the police, and a brief mention of the delicate subject of corruption. However, there is no set pattern to fraud investigation. Virtually every fraud investigation is different and it is not possible to devise a comprehensive set of rules which can be applied in all circumstances. The auditor must still use his own judgement and intuition.

Auditor's responsibility for fraud

The CIPFA statement on the role and objectives of internal audit recognises that part of the responsibility of internal audit in a public authority is 'to review, appraise and report upon the extent to which the organisation's assets and interests are accounted for and safeguarded from losses of all kinds arising from *fraud and other offences* and waste, extravagance and inefficient administration, poor value for money and other cause'.

The CIPFA *Statements on Internal Audit Practice – Public Sector* contain a specific item on irregularities and fraud, namely:

> The internal auditor shall endeavour to reveal any serious defect in systems of internal control which might lead to the perpetration of fraud and must have regard to the possibility of malpractice in areas under examination. He shall be alert to the possibility of corruption and be prepared to inform the appropriate level of management of any justifiable suspicions.

The line taken by CIPFA, that internal audit has some responsibility for the prevention and detection of fraud, is not a universally accepted view and some auditors argue that, because fraud occurs generally as a result of deficiencies in systems of internal control, then the management responsible for those deficiencies should undertake the investigation. Whilst the authors subscribe to the view that fraud occurs because of weaknesses in internal control systems, they cannot accept that it is management's responsibility to investigate it. In their opinion, internal audit should conduct such investigations, and a failure to do so is an abrogation of *part* of its role and objectives.

If fraud comes to light during an audit investigation, then it is internal audit's job to investigate it and, if need be, to refer it to the police. Similarly, when there are rumours of a possible fraud, internal audit has a duty to investigate.

Attitudes to fraud

Once it has been established that a fraud has been committed, an important consideration in any fraud investigation is to decide on the line to be taken. There is one line which says 'the least said, the better' and which seeks to avoid any risk of the sort of adverse publicity which court proceedings are likely to attract. A more forthright attitude for management to adopt, particularly in the public sector, is to accept that it is the duty of any citizen to report criminal activities to the police and to expect the due processes of law to follow. In fact, the Criminal Law Act 1967 makes it a general offence to act with the intention of impeding the apprehension or prosecution of offenders for arrestable offences without lawful authority or reasonable excuse.

However, the circumstances of a fraud must be taken into account in considering whether to refer the matter to the police. A public authority may be justified in not referring a case where the amount stolen is small, or where there are other mitigating factors, such as illness of the perpetrator. As a general rule, however, most frauds in the public sector should be referred to the police who should decide on prosecution. Furthermore, it should be noted that it is often a condition of fidelity guarantee insurance policies that the police are informed of frauds.

Fraud statistics

Fraud statistics are not available for the whole of the public sector, but, in the local government field, an analysis of reported frauds, issued by the former Chief Inspector of Audit, shows that the total amount in England and Wales over the three years 1981/82 to 1983/84 (the latest available figures) was £1,288,928, an average of £429,643 per annum. The total amounts involved over the three years were as follows:

1981/82	£456,000
1982/83	£494,455
1983/84	£338,473

In 1983/84, 31 of the 65 frauds were for amounts over £2,500, compared with 28 in 1982/83. Eighteen were over £5,000, eleven of which were in excess of

£10,000. An analysis of the frauds over services showed the following to be the most vulnerable in 1983/84:

	Number
Education	15
Housing	8
Leisure	8
Technical	6
Finance	6

Eleven of the 1983/84 frauds were in existence for over three years.

Almost 38 per cent of the total losses in 1983/84 was recovered by way of refund from, or on behalf of, the defaulters. After further recoveries under fidelity insurance policies and from superannuation refunds, there remained about £41,000 unrecovered.

It is not likely that all discovered cases were reported to the Audit Commission and there must be many borderline cases which were not classified as fraud. Furthermore, the published statistics show frauds only over £500. Undoubtedly, some frauds remain undiscovered. Nevertheless, when compared with total local government income and expenditure for England and Wales of over £30,000 million per annum, it is apparent that the total amount lost as the direct result of fraud is a very small percentage. However, one must not be too complacent, since a very high standard of financial stewardship is expected in the public sector.

Types of fraud

The authors have analysed three distinct categories of fraud, as follows:

1. Basic frauds.
2. Wider expenditure frauds.
3. Corruption.

Each category will be discussed in turn.

Basic frauds

Basic frauds arise primarily because of a breakdown in systems. The following constitute basic frauds:

1. *Income*. The retention or the misappropriation of cash is the simplest and most usual type of fraud. Examples include the misappropriation of collections, rents, school meal monies and car parking fees. Income frauds can, as a general rule, be detected by the careful monitoring of the regularity of banking. In the authors' view, it is not audit's responsibility to monitor the regularity of banking on a routine basis. This should be the role of a Central Income Section, which could usefully employ a computerised system to monitor actual receipts from accountable officers, units, establishments, etc. against a predetermined norm on a weekly basis and to highlight significant deviations.
2. *Minor expenditure*. This involves fictitious payments, purchases and petty

cash payments. Frauds occurring in this area arise because of weaknesses in internal control. Recent examples of such frauds include the falsification of pension refund vouchers, fictitious vouchers for the payment of interview expenses and submission of false invoices.

3. *False wages/salary claims*. These are a common occurrence in the public sector, but many examples of frauds which have arisen in this area have occurred because of a violation of the principles of internal check. Examples include overclaimed overtime, falsification of time sheets through inflation of hours worked and fictitious sessional fee claims.
4. *Bonus schemes*. These are worthy of special mention because they are so frequent. It is unusual for an internal audit section not to discover a fraud in this area.
5. *Theft of equipment and stores*. This is an area often neglected by everyone, including internal audit. Inventories may be out of date (assuming they exist), and frequently security arrangements are only related to break-ins and may not cover the possibility of theft by employees. In such circumstances, employees may be able to steal equipment and stores almost with impunity, whilst the petty cash is well protected. Typical frauds of this nature are theft of car spares from Transport Depots, theft of materials (such as paint, wood, fittings, etc.) from direct labour units and theft of valuable exhibits from museums.
6. *Falsification of travelling and subsistence claims*. These are fairly common occurrences for internal audit to investigate. Once again, any frauds occurring generally arise from a breakdown in internal control, with the person responsible for certifying the claim not checking it properly.
7. *Computer frauds*. As far as is known, the public sector has not experienced a major fraud in this area. However, two incidents demonstrate that basic frauds can still occur in this area. One involved a failure to account for income arising from the use of the computer. A second one involved the manipulation of overtime payments in the Computer Control Section.

It should be stressed that many types of fraud are very basic and occur because of a breakdown or weakness in financial systems. No one person should have sole control of a financial transaction, yet, when one examines a system where fraud has occurred, this is often just the case.

Wider expenditure frauds

Moving from the more basic frauds to wider aspects, one of the biggest areas for possible fraud is in the supply of goods and services to public sector organisations. Yet this is an area to which auditors direct little attention. Internal audit can review the expenditure side, and such reviews can be most enlightening and rewarding.

Just spend a couple of minutes considering the huge amount of goods and services purchased in your organisation, such as heating fuel, petrol, food supplies, vehicle spares, building maintenance and stationery supplies, furniture and equipment. After the contracts have been awarded it is worth asking the following questions:

1. What controls are employed to see that the correct quality and quantity of goods are supplied?
2. What checks are made regarding a possible 'ring' of contractors?
3. Who delivers the items contained within the contract – is it the firm who was awarded the contract?
4. Are company searches on firms on approved tender lists carried out to establish whether any links exist between the various firms or even that the organisation's employees are recorded as directors?
5. How much work is undertaken by internal audit on an examination of the receipt of tenders?
6. What controls are in evidence over price increases in, for example, food contracts?

Corruption

An investigation into the supply of goods and services leads into the delicate area of corruption. The authors believe that many auditors are complacent about this, despite events of the past few years where significant public figures have been connected or implicated in major corruption offences, and despite two publications. The *Salmon Report on Standards of Conduct in Public Life* was published in 1976 and an article on the Salmon Report by the Nationalised Industries Chief Internal Auditors' Group appeared in *Public Finance and Accountancy* in August 1979.

It is absolutely vital that the auditor is aware of the possibility of corruption when undertaking his investigations. Although fairly obvious, it is important that the auditor takes the following items of evidence into consideration where corruption is concerned:

1. Rumours of a manager living beyond his means.
2. Tales of high living.
3. Frequent visits to the office by certain contractors to see a manager.
4. Car registration details.
5. Indication (from an examination of travelling claims) of frequent visits to a contractor by a manager.

Practical aspects of fraud investigation

It has already been stressed that there is no set pattern to a fraud investigation. The auditor must use his own judgement and intuition. He must also act on 'tip-offs' and rumours – there is a tendency for personnel to inform the auditor and then abrogate responsibility. The auditor cannot afford to ignore such information, however scant; to do so could cause serious problems, particularly if fraud were detected sometime later. However, it must be borne in mind that anonymous statements are sometimes made for malicious reasons. Time, patience and planning are particularly important in any fraud investigations. Auditors should not rush into an investigation since one of the great dangers is in alerting the guilty party.

The auditor's task is to investigate and establish fraud and ascertain its extent. This work can, without doubt, be undertaken more efficiently if the procedures to be followed are defined in advance. Unless investigations are conducted carefully and in a disciplined way, an oversight or transgression may occur which, at a later point of the enquiry, could at least be embarrassing or at worst prevent the successful prosecution or dismissal of a defaulter.

These considerations apply to the conduct of a fraud investigation, no matter how the irregularity comes to the auditor's notice. If it is brought to light by a third party, however, the auditor's first step must be to check the alleged facts. This must be done as soon as possible, but not before all the relevant information relating to the offender and his responsibilities has been assembled. The procedure is similar to the preparation for an audit visit and, in fact, such investigations are frequently carried out in the guise of a normal audit. It is desirable that two auditors should be present at all stages of a fraud investigation.

Where the auditor is satisfied that there are grounds for thinking that a fraud has been committed he should do the following:

1. Carefully check the facts again.
2. Restrict questioning to establishing that the suspicion appears to be well founded.
3. Retain all records which may be involved, bearing in mind when handling documents that finger-printing or other forensic examination may take place later.
4. Establish all the areas of activity of the person under suspicion in order to establish the potential size of the fraud.
5. If necessary, telephone the audit manager to inform him of the facts and to seek guidance. This call should be made from an outside telephone.

At this early stage it is important to establish a file for the investigation. All material should be assembled chronologically, and a dated index of progress should be maintained, together with detailed notes of all relevant interviews, meetings and decisions taken. In maintaining this file, auditors should be aware that it may become evidence in a court of law or at an industrial tribunal considering an appeal against unfair dismissal.

The objectives of the investigation will be as follows:

1. To collect sufficient evidence to prove the offence and to identify the defaulter.
2. To have the employee suspended while a full investigation is completed.
3. To provide evidence for disciplinary or legal action.

It is not possible to detail the work needed to achieve the foregoing – the circumstances of each case will dictate what is needed. However, the auditor must be particularly alert to ascertain the full extent of the fraud and any related frauds; he must be painstaking and particularly careful, bearing in mind that his action or omissions may subsequently be very carefully examined in a court of law or an industrial tribunal.

Relationship with police

At this stage, it is worth stressing that it is extremely useful for the audit manager to build up an effective liaison between the police and the audit section. This relationship is vital and there must be close co-operation and a great deal of trust. With it, both can gain a great deal. It would be useful to establish a relationship with the Fraud Squad at Police Headquarters, rather than the local divisional office, although some auditors have found the latter very useful.

If such a link is established, the expertise of the police, on an informal basis, is available to the auditor in planning the course of an investigation into a potential fraud. It is possible to discuss with the police the facts which are available, without having to ask them to investigate the matter. In addition, it may be that the police can produce some information, or at least suggest you acquire certain items to assist you. Certainly, the value of the advice of the police should not be underrated. It is also possible to overcome the problem of deciding when a case should be referred to the police and, in particular, in deciding whether audit should interview the suspect first (or even at all) before handing the case over to the police.

The question of how soon the police should be informed officially is always a difficult problem. In theory, the police should be informed as soon as there are reasonable grounds for suspecting that a criminal offence has been committed. In practice, it is a matter for local judgement, based on the facts of each individual case, but the informal relationship mentioned earlier can be of great assistance. However, for general guidance, the following are suggested times to inform the police:

1. Straight away – when there are suspicions of corrupt practice.
2. Before interviews take place – when there is some evidence of systematic theft, but it needs to be confirmed by witnessed observation if the case is to be made for criminal prosecution.
3. As soon as fraud has been established – when the defaulter cannot be identified from the accounting records (e.g. fraudulent encashment of a cheque).
4. Probably after the first interview – when the records indicate fraud by a particular person. It is useful to have the interview to confirm the evidence of the records and to suspend the offender while further enquiries are made.

In deciding when to involve the police, it must be remembered that the auditor, however much he would like to, should not take over the role of the police to 'obtain' a confession. The police are skilled interrogators and should be brought in as soon as circumstances warrant it.

It is appropriate to mention briefly the area of surveillance. As a general rule, this should be done by the police but, from time to time, internal audit needs to undertake some observation before the police are involved, either formally or informally. Where the surveillance is undertaken in order to provide evidence, it is vital that the original notes of the observations are recorded, signed and dated immediately by the person making them. Records should be kept of all the details noted or checks undertaken. It is also useful to warn the police before undertaking surveillance work to avoid the embarrassment of auditors being reported for suspicious activity! Finally, a man and woman from internal audit looks far less obvious than two men when surveillance is being undertaken!

Planning and conducting the interview

When it has been decided, or circumstances dictate, that the auditor will have to interview the suspect during the course of a fraud investigation, then it is useful to undertake some careful planning beforehand. Basically there are three stages – before the interview, during the interview and after it – and each is considered in turn.

Before conducting an interview, the auditor should consider the following points:

1. The aspects on which information is required. An approach is to prepare the questions in advance of the interview. This has much to commend it since it presents a structured plan of action. However, if this is done, the auditor must realise that supplementary questions may need to be asked during the interview. If the questions are not written in advance, then at least a written check list is required.
2. The time and place for the interview must be fixed, bearing in mind the need to avoid any interruptions. If there is a break in a formal interview, the interviewee might take advantage of it to fabricate an explanation, destroy evidence or even 'tip-off' a colleague. Formal interviews tend to be quite lengthy, and clearly it is important to avoid the discussion going beyond normal working hours, otherwise the interviewee might justifiably refuse to continue. Consequently a late start should be avoided and, as a general rule, the best time and place to hold a formal interview is either early in the morning or immediately after lunch at a location away from the interviewee's normal place of work.
3. The people who will be present. It is important to have as few people as possible present whilst, at the same time, ensuring that all interested parties are represented. Two auditors should be present, mainly to ensure that a reliable witness to the proceedings is available. As a general rule, one auditor should ask the questions and the second should make such notes as are necessary. It may be useful to have a manager from the interviewee's department present who has the power to suspend the employee if necessary.
4. The interviewee should be advised of the time and place of the interview and given a very brief indication about the matter to be discussed. However, the auditor should not be too specific about this for the obvious reason of not helping the suspect to devise a defence or to destroy evidence.
5. The interviewee may ask to be accompanied by a 'friend' who may be a representative from the union. This practice seems to be increasing; however, at this stage, the advice would be for the auditor to resist it since he is only seeking explanations – it is not a formal disciplinary hearing. However, if the request is conceded, then it must be under the strict understanding that the 'friend' is present as an observer only.

The following are some useful hints on procedure at the actual interview:

1. As a general rule, one auditor should ask the questions and the second should make notes.
2. It is vital that nothing is done at the interview which could be construed as duress by the interviewee. No statement by an accused person is admissible in evidence against him unless it can be shown by the prosecution to have been made voluntarily. Consequently, the auditor must not make any threats or promises, actual or implied, in order to obtain a statement.
3. The auditor should make it clear to the interviewee that it is he who is conducting the interview. This may be difficult if a senior person is present from the employee's department, but it is a point worth resolving in advance.
4. It may be useful to begin the interview by asking the interviewee to outline his understanding of his duties and responsibilities in connection with the matter under review. It needs to be established whether the duties were explained to the interviewee and, if so, by whom. Any such statement should be carefully noted and may provide a useful base for subsequent disciplinary action.
5. Great skill and care must be exercised in framing questions. Making statements should be avoided since the objective is to concentrate on asking questions in order to obtain answers. Any evasive answers must be followed up by supplementary questions. It is important that the auditor covers all the ground to be discussed at the interview without the need for adjournments which could be used to advantage by the interviewee.
6. If two or more people are implicated in a potential fraud, then it is imperative that the auditors prevent them from making contact between individual interviews and creating alibis.
7. If, during the course of an interview, the auditor forms the opinion that he has reasonable grounds for believing the interviewee has committed an offence, or if the interviewee admits to an offence, then it is the time to conclude the interview. The suspect should not be pressed to make a statement because the police will be able to do that more effectively and, if they are to consider prosecution, they will prefer to take the statement themselves.
8. The suspect might insist on making a statement, however, and, in this case, he should be allowed to do so. It is imperative that the auditor is familiar with the application of the Judges' Rules so that the statement obtained is admissible as evidence in court.* Under such circumstances, the auditor must apply the caution in the following terms:

   > 'You are not obliged to say anything unless you wish to do so, but what you say may be put into writing and given in evidence.'

   The Rules continue, as follows:

   > 'When, after being cautioned, a person is being questioned, or elects to make a statement, a record shall be kept of the time and place at which any such questioning or statement began and ended and of the persons present.'

* It should be noted that the Judges' Rules do not apply in Scotland. However, they do form a useful guideline for Scottish auditors.

The statement *must* be given on a voluntary basis and not as a result of any real or implied threat or promise. It is suggested that the statement begins with a paragraph such as the following:

> 'I make this statement of my own free will. I have been told that I need not say anything unless I wish to do so and that whatever I say may be given in evidence.'

When the statement has been completed, it should be signed and the signature must be witnessed.

9. Where no written statement is taken from a suspect during an interview, the auditor's notes have the potential of becoming important evidence if criminal charges result. The auditor should keep this in mind when taking and writing up the notes which should be agreed, signed and dated by both auditors as soon as possible after the interview.
10. At the conclusion of the interview, the auditor must make sure that he obtains possession of any original documents which may be required as evidence. Finally, he must be aware that the security of audit working papers is absolutely crucial. This may sound obvious, but a case was reported of a fraud investigation where the audit working papers and notes were left out overnight. They disappeared; so did the fraud investigation!

It is quite easy for an auditor to forget some of the actions that are required to be taken after an interview which has produced reasonable grounds for believing that fraud has occurred. Some vital actions are as follows:

1. *Suspension*. This should be the final decision at the conclusion of the interview, and normally an employee will be suspended on full pay, but it might be possible to arrange a suspension without pay. Of course, it is not the role of the auditor to suspend, but that of line management. If the employee admits to a fraud, then instant dismissal may be a possibility.
2. *Leaving the building*. The offender should be accompanied from the interview back to his place of work to collect, under supervision, any personal belongings. It is vital that records which might assist the subsequent investigation are not removed or destroyed. The offender should be escorted off the premises and allowed no further access without the approval of the auditor in charge of the investigation.
3. *Informing the police*. The police need to be informed of the outcome of the interview as a matter of urgency.
4. *Dismissal*. In order to minimise the increasing loss to the organisation represented by suspension pay, dismissal should be considered as soon as there are adequate grounds. This can be done before any criminal prosecution is made, and, possibly, in large or complex frauds, even before the full extent of the loss is known.
5. *Insurance*. It is normally a requirement that the insurers are informed of the possibility of a claim.
6. *Recovery of loss*. It may be possible, in certain circumstances, to recover the amount of any loss from the appropriate pension fund. In local government, the external auditors have powers to declare amounts due where losses have occurred through wilful misconduct. In criminal courses, it is possible to ask the court to make an order for restitution.

7. *Informing the external auditor.* Internal audit should make the external auditor aware of the fraud immediately (and vice versa). Whichever auditor is involved should inform his counterpart in order to prevent duplication of effort, to exchange relevant information and to prevent any difficulties which could arise if the other auditor did, possibly coincidentally, have any reason to become involved with the suspect concerning the fraud or some other unrelated matter.
8. *System review.* A full investigation of the circumstances surrounding the fraudulent occurrences must be undertaken, the system must be evaluated and proposals for strengthening it (if a system weakness is found) must be agreed upon and implemented.
9. *Recording of irregularities.* As part of the management of the audit section, a record file of irregularities should be maintained.

Conclusion

'Honesty is frequent and dull; fraud is rare but stimulating', some people say. Fraud investigation is perhaps the most exciting and exacting aspect of audit work. Any investigation must, therefore, be conducted with the utmost tact and with a determination to establish the facts and bring the matter to a conclusion as soon as possible. All frauds are different and the need for flexibility in approach during an investigation is of paramount importance, and a high degree of urgency is required of the investigating officer.

CHAPTER 9

The auditor and value for money

Value for money is an extremely wide-ranging topic, with implications for every activity undertaken by any organisation. This chapter is restricted to a discussion of the role of the auditor in regard to this.

Definition of value for money

It is almost impossible to produce a definition of value for money that will satisfy everyone's interpretation. Such is the nature of the concept that definitions range from 'the cheapest unit cost' at one end of the scale to 'the best possible quality' at the other. In the authors' view, value for money must encompass a balance between input and output. Implicit in this is a pre-specification of the level of output (i.e. service) that is required, and value for money represents achieving that level of output at the most economical cost. It follows, therefore, that the lowest unit cost does not always represent the best value for money and, indeed, the cheapest solution is rarely the best.

Responsibility for value for money

Everyone associated with an organisation has some responsibility for value for money, from the office boy to the chief executive; however, it must be said that the prime responsibility lies with management. If poor value for money exists in a department, the blame must lie with the departmental manager, not the auditor. It follows, therefore, that the auditor's role must be to assist management in its responsibility. It must be stressed that the achievement of value for money relies heavily upon the right *attitude* being present at all levels in the organisation. Management's aim should be to encourage an environment which is conducive to optimum value for money. Unless the people working for an organisation genuinely want to achieve value for money, then all the systems and procedures in the world will be to no avail.

Structural organisation

Some audit managers, particularly in the field of internal audit, have set up separate teams to deal with value for money. These enjoy a splendid range of grandiose titles, such as 'Cost Effectiveness Unit', 'Value Review Team' and 'Management Audit Group'. The objective has been to set aside staff with a particular aptitude for value-for-money work and, in so doing, to create a team which will develop experience and expertise in this field, unencumbered with the more routine aspects of audit work. This approach has worked well in many organisations, but, set against its undoubted benefits, there must be a number of disadvantages:

1. The value-for-money specialist will not have the detailed knowledge of the 'service auditor' and thus it may take longer to carry out the necessary research work.
2. Valuable departmental contacts built up by the 'service auditor' may not be available to the value-for-money team.
3. The creation of what may be regarded as an élite value-for-money team may have a demoralising effect on the audit staff who are not selected to be members of that team.

In many audit sections, value-for-money work is seen as an integral part of the audit task, and a separate allocation of time is not thought to be appropriate. Auditors are required to have regard to value-for-money issues, whilst conducting systems-based and transaction-based audits. In other organisations, a separate allocation is made for value-for-money studies, and individual exercises are planned. In this way, the audit manager can be sure that specific attention is directed to the need to achieve value for money and resources can be concentrated upon areas of known poor performance which, incidentally, may well have been identified during systems-based and transaction-based audits.

The three Es

Any serious student of audit will know that 'the three Es' – economy, efficiency and effectiveness – are the three pillars of value for money. The auditor's role in regard to the first two is rarely challenged. Who would argue that the auditor has a duty to ensure that resources are acquired as economically as possible and that those resources are then used in the most efficient manner? However, it is when the auditor becomes involved in 'effectiveness' that he may encounter problems. When he begins to question how effective an organisation's policies are in achieving its defined objectives he may well meet with resistance; yet, if the auditor is to meet the objectives set out in Chapter 1, he must question the effectiveness of policies.

Logically, the auditor's approach to value for money should be to determine what the objectives of the organisation are – not the easiest of tasks with many public sector bodies. He must then ascertain the policies which have been adopted to achieve those objectives. Generally this will be an easier task as public sector organisations are notorious policy-makers – a cynic might say that it is often the policies which dictate the objectives, rather than the reverse. The auditor's task then involves an appraisal of the effectiveness of those policies and the economy and efficiency with which they are carried out.

The auditor's role

It has already been stated that the prime responsibility for ensuring that value for money is achieved rests firmly with management. The auditor's role is to review the systems which management use to monitor value for money and to ensure that positive and effective action is taken whenever poor value for money is identified. Up to this point the role is common to both the internal auditor and his external counterpart. However, the internal auditor is much more likely to develop a role beyond this stage. Aside from the 'systems' approach to value for money, auditors will often become involved in value-for-money projects. Such projects can conveniently be broken down into five distinct stages, as follows:

1. The identification of an area where, *prima facie*, there is evidence of poor value for money.
2. The detailed investigation of that area to establish the facts.
3. The development of proposals to remedy the situation.
4. The implementation of those proposals.
5. Monitoring the success of the remedy.

Whilst it could never be argued that the first stage is the sole responsibility of the auditor (indeed, everyone has a part to play in this), no one would dispute that the auditor has a function to fulfil in this respect and, in many ways, is ideally suited to carry out that function. So far as the second stage is concerned, arrangements will vary, but there is no doubt that the detailed knowledge built up by the auditor, together with his investigative skills, will enable him to assist considerably at this stage. It is not advisable that the auditor should become involved in the third stage, as to do so could jeopardise his future independence. An auditor would certainly be reluctant to criticise the lack of success of any proposals with which he was associated. However, where management's resources are so restricted or its investigative skills so limited as to render impossible the development of suitable solutions to the problems, then the auditor may find it necessary to assist. However, even in such extreme cases, he should ensure that management agrees with the proposals, and that they are regarded by the organisation as having been developed by management. The fourth stage is purely a matter for management and the auditor should not become involved. As far as monitoring is concerned, the responsibility must, again, lie largely with management, but there is no doubt that the auditor has a duty to ensure that management carries out this task, and perhaps one effective way of doing this is to monitor the success of the remedy personally.

Value review systems

Apart from the more common management accounting and costing systems, many additional procedures exist to assist management, and thus to assist the auditor to identify poor value for money. In a general publication of this nature, it is not appropriate to discuss these in depth; indeed, each one could merit a publication of its own. However, it will be helpful to identify some systems and to discuss briefly the extent to which they may be of use to the auditor. The more common systems are as follows:

1. *Performance review committees.* Few organisations operate these committees as they often degenerate into a vehicle for members to attack heads of spending departments. CIPFA produced an interesting publication in 1977 entitled *Performance Review in the Public Sector and the Role of the Audit in the Process* which provided a practical scenario within which such a committee could be developed, and explained the auditor's role in the process.
2. *Comparative studies and statistics.* Many managers, particularly in the public sector, avoid comparative studies and statistics and yet these must provide one of the most useful means of concentrating scarce investigatory resources into potentially lucrative areas. Certainly the auditor needs to remember that comparative statistics take no account of variations in sources of information, differing levels of service or of environmental factors which will, in many cases, undoubtedly account for differing costs. He must simply regard such statistics as a useful means of focusing his attention on areas which *may* prove to be beneficial. The use of comparative statistics need not be restricted to comparisons between organisations. Comparisons between similar units within an organisation, or from year to year in the same unit, are equally useful. Comparative studies are a natural development from comparative statistics. Where unit costs are found to differ considerably, then it becomes necessary to study the differences in depth and to identify the causes. It is only in this way that a meaningful conclusion can be reached.
3. *Selected invoices*. Some organisations operate a system whereby a limited number of invoices are selected, at random or otherwise, and are subjected to detailed scrutiny, often by the auditor. Members are often involved in this process, which has the benefit of creating an environment where any invoice has the potential of coming under the microscope. In organisations that operate a system such as this, the certification of invoices ceases to be the automatic, robot-like process which it can sometimes become.
4. *Budgets and budgetary control.* It is often argued that budgets and budgetary control, as they impose a cash constraint, play a major part in the development of value for money. Conversely, it can be argued with equal conviction that incremental budgeting, combined with the annual year-end 'binge' to spend up to the target and thus protect next year's allocation, has precisely the opposite effect. One of the most useful exercises which an auditor can undertake is to 'audit the estimates'. In other words, to examine the system by which the estimates are compiled and to 'zero the base' on selected budget heads and rebuild the budget on a 'needs' rather than an 'incremental' basis.

Incentives to value for money

Many examples are available of areas where special value-for-money studies have produced considerable benefits and savings. A useful catalogue of such exercises has been compiled by CIPFA and was published in 1982 under the title of *Local Government Value for Money Handbook*. A study of many such exercises reveals that a key factor in the success of many value-for-money proposals lies in incentive. As already emphasised, attitudes play a major part in the achievement of value for money, and the provision of incentive does much to create the right attitudes. In an era of cutbacks and retrenchment, programme area managers may well be better disposed to co-operating in value-for-money studies if a proportion of the resultant savings is fed back into their programme areas in the form of real growth.

CHAPTER 10

Review and measurement of audit performance

The subject of the review and measurement of audit performance has, until recently, received scant attention. In Chapter 4, the quantitative control of the audit function was dealt with and, in this chapter, the qualitative aspects will be covered. The issue has been approached from the following points of view:

1. The newly appointed audit manager who conducts an initial assessment of his section.
2. The audit manager of long standing who keeps the section under review.
3. The external auditor who is called upon to comment on the adequacy of internal audit, which is a statutory requirement in local government in England and Wales.
4. The Chief Executive or Board Member for Finance, or even a committee which conducts a review of the internal audit activity.

Auditors need to know how well they are doing and the audit manager needs some measure of the success (or otherwise) of his own unit for confidence, defence and effective management. He needs to develop an intelligence and information system to inform him of what is going on, and a control network to enable progress to be monitored and objectives met. It is relatively easy to describe general internal audit objectives. It is not so easy to translate such goals and aspirations into standards and targets. Nor is it a simple task to measure audit output in qualitative terms. Furthermore, the auditor's aims and work are, to a degree, influenced by the expectations of others.

The need for yardsticks

Apart from any professional edicts, statements of objectives and output are essential for the purposes of management and control. As he is in control, the audit manager needs to establish objectives and standards, monitor performance against purpose, and plan, establish and investigate any perceived variations and select and implement corrective action.

There are a number of reasons why audit performance should be measured, as follows:

1. To gain assurance that the audit team is meeting the objectives set by management.

2. To ensure that expensive resources (staff) are being used effectively and value for money is being obtained.
3. To ensure compliance with statutory obligations.
4. To ensure that quality of performance is of a high standard.
5. To promote staff motivation within internal audit through regular assessment and feedback.
6. To see that internal audit is not 'outside' reviews which operate in the other sections of the organisation.
7. To gauge the cost of internal audit. (This may be questioned as a 'non-productive overhead', particularly during a recession.)
8. To ensure that external auditors assess the adequacy of internal audit.

Where possible, events and expectations should be quantified. The difficulty arises over the extent to which internal audit's work and output can be measured – especially its quality. The problems of measurement of service output are not unique to audit; however, matters are complicated by the less than universal agreement as to the precise nature and purpose of internal audit. Certain measures proposed, therefore, are not only impracticable but also invalid.

There are two further issues closely related to the development of performance yardsticks, as follows:

1. *Assessing the quality of internal audit.* This involves the need for quality control, quality assurance and the audit of audit.
2. *Comparing the audit performance against standards.* This involves the consideration of both current practices (the 'state of the art') and what *should* be the case (in terms of objectives, conditions for success and what is deemed 'adequate').

Although managerial responsibility is the prime reason for developing performance measures, the audit manager needs, not only to demonstrate to himself the level of performance, but also to convince others. If there is any question mark over the quality of performance, particularly, then the obligations of accountability, the requirement for independent review, and the need to demonstrate one's worth in reacting to the various pressures, make the development of some form of performance assessment an urgent task for most audit managers.

Who should review?

Two sources of review, not necessarily mutually exclusive, can be identified – in-house and external.

In-house reviews

Internal assessment is necessary for reasons of day-to-day control, revision of purpose and direction, annual report, and line accountability. In addition to need, there are obvious advantages of internal inspection; however, outsiders might doubt their objectivity or request disclosure. In-house reviews might be conducted by the newly appointed audit manager, the long-established audit manager, or executive management.

External reviews

External reviews should be performed by qualified persons who are independent of the organisation. Such reviews bring the benefits of objectivity, and comparative and specialist knowledge. They might be conducted by external auditors, consultants or a central inspectorate.

By far the most common reviewer is the external auditor who may be obliged, under statute, to review the adequacy of internal audit. Consultants, in the form of an accountancy firm or a team of management consultants, might be useful to gain extra status if they point to conditions which adversely affect internal audit performance. A third external agency is some form of inspectorate. The Treasury, for example, has such a unit to monitor internal audit within central government.

How might reviews be conducted?

As with all audits, there are two basic approaches which can be adopted, as follows:

1. *The substantive approach.* This results in the expression of an opinion of audit's performance.
2. *The procedural approach.* This examines those systems and factors which promote or affect audit operations.

The substantive approach has two aspects, as follows:

1. *Negative.* This points out matters arising and indicates inefficiencies, failures and inadequacies.
2. *Positive.* A statement of the overall efficiency and effectiveness of internal audit, indicating its successes, benefits and results.

The procedural approach is again two-fold, as follows:

1. *Negative.* This indicates factors which inhibit effective audit performance, e.g. lack of independence, non-audit tasks and inadequate training.
2. *Positive.* This examines those controls and influences which promote effective auditing, e.g. the application of management principles, internal controls and procedures, and support.

Reviews should adopt a basic audit methodology: the acquisition of evidence, comparison of findings against internal and external standards, and the evaluation of adequacy of controls and performance. This raises once more the question of the desirable level of performance and the degree of adequacy. The end opinion will, to some extent, be a matter of judgement and qualification.

Possible measures of performance

The constant quest for precision tends to result in a search for quantitative measures. Given, however, the nature of the service and the difficulty of measuring quality, many reviews in practice concentrate on qualitative assessment – examining procedures and progress, rather than results. The various means which have been suggested, and which are examined in this chapter, reflect both approaches. They are as follows:

1. *Costs.* These are a measure of input only; yet resources need to be controlled, budgets set and met, and costs established and kept within reason. However, effective budgetary control is no measure of performance.
2. *Factors which affect performance.* The scrutiny of internal processes and external conditions, the enthusiasm of management, the degree of compliance with standards, and other factors are useful indicators; but as indicators they are guides not measures, and constitute no proof of adequate performance. 'Bad' practices can lead to good results and vice versa. Too much time can be spent on administration. Adverse conditions can be used as excuses. But as a base, most assessments will include consideration of such factors and may indicate the underlying causes of inadequacies. Initially, of course, we must determine what is meant by 'performance'.
3. *Progress against plan.* This is, at best, an activity measure. As with the factors which affect performance, it is really only a process indicator, related neither to quality nor service. However, such an indicator reflects commitment and industry (which are only as good as one's original intentions), and perhaps audit presence, not result, is sufficient (if one believes in deterrence).
4. *Activity levels.* Checking the number of establishments visited, the levels of expenditure covered and the mileage clocked up is obviously only a measure of quantity. The nettle of determining true output has yet to be grasped.
5. *Reporting success.* This measure includes the number and length of reports, points made, and the number of recommendations made, accepted, implemented and successfully executed.
6. *Frauds found.* Such a measure has an obvious impact on auditors, auditees and management. But what does it prove? It could be argued that it is a measure of failure to cite the number of frauds detected. Consequently, it might be better to cite the number of frauds prevented, or the number of successful prosecutions as the result of fraud investigations.

   Under this heading, the following questions need to be considered:

   (a) Whether this measure reflects the true aim of audit.
   (b) Whether deterrence can be measured.
   (c) Whether this is a fair measure, not being a controllable factor.
   (d) Whether audit is on a hiding to nothing, in that fraud is so difficult to detect.
   (e) Whether the true extent of fraud detected is measurable.
   (f) Whether the figures are meaningful if recoveries and insurance are taken into account.
7. *Savings made.* There are theoretical and practical arguments against using savings, economies or recoveries as measures, despite their obvious popularity.

8. *Achievements.* These are audits' successes but these are not always quantifiable nor tangible.
9. *Absence of criticism.* Is audit successful if it avoids censure and critical comment? Certainly a high number of abortive projects, recommendations not acted upon, and complaints can indicate that something is amiss. Alternatively, is the number of complaints a measure of success?
10. *User satisfaction.* This is perhaps a reflection of the confidence in, or respect for, audit. This measure quantifies the number of queries handled, the number of requests responded to, the number of uncritical reports, the areas handled per auditor, the number of staff against turnover and the costs per man-day.
11. *Comparisons.* This measure includes the comparisons of practices, scope, objectives, etc., with other similar organisations; of man-days spent against target; of staff against establishment; and of this year's performance with last year's. The ultimate comparison, however, is of actual performance and achievement with expectations, intentions and standards – internal or external.

The approach

The means available to those assessing audit performance – observation of procedures and results, inspection of records, interviewing of staff and other means – are also available to all auditors.

The use of questionnaires is a common means of acquiring evidence. The use of an internal control questionnaire on assessing the adequacy of internal audit is an ideal method for auditor managers to use. (A specimen questionnaire is set out in Appendix 4.) Similarly, the external auditor often uses a questionnaire approach, and an example, geared to adherence to CIPFA statements, is set out in Appendix 5.

In addition to satisfying himself about the answers to the above questions, the 'reviewer' should also look at certain measures of success. For example, he should want to see the extent to which 'audit findings' emerge from completed regularity and systems audits and the extent to which audit recommendations have been adopted by management. He should assess the level of success achieved by audit in the field of value for money and the extent of 'savings' resulting from audit recommendations. He should also want to determine the amount of fraud and corruption which has been identified and to assess how well the audit section has dealt with this.

What is important is to adopt a healthy attitude to any review of audit. It is easy to be critical of the reviewer, to adopt a defensive posture and to cover up deficiencies.

If audits of audit are conducted, they must be done well. To get the right answers, the right questions must be asked. Appraisals should be depersonalised – evaluation of the effectiveness of internal audit should not be linked directly with the performance appraisal of individuals.

It is easy to be obsessed with the problem of performance measurement. It is far better to be rationally subjective, and admit to such, than to put excess effort in the search for quantified measures, to claim or appear to be wholly objective, or to use spurious measures.

No one measure is adequate, nor sufficient. Evaluation should be based upon a composite of measures, a mix of objective study and value judgement. Ideally, any evaluation should consider the whole range of performance, from resource use to value, and take into account all benefits and contributions, and all costs – financial, opportunity and social. However, measures should be simple, intelligible, and, above all, usable.

Equally, it may be appropriate to break down the audit objectives and develop a series of measures or indicators accordingly. In this way, yardsticks could be developed for planned and unprogrammed work – for success in the areas of EDP, fraud and cost reduction, and for value in terms of providing advice and protection, dealing with queries, launching initiatives or stimulating change. One note of caution – measuring an activity legitimises it and encourages its future development.

Conclusion

Whilst the review of audit performance as a single exercise, conducted by a new audit manager, has been dealt with, it must be said that, in practice, such a review is very much an ongoing process. Certainly a new audit manager should conduct a comprehensive review upon his appointment, external audit will conduct occasional comprehensive reviews of internal audit, and there should be a system of independent comprehensive reviews of audit by, for example the chief executive, but these should not detract from the audit manager's duty to keep the audit function under constant review.

It should be stressed that this ongoing review cannot be conducted solely from behind the audit manager's desk. Many of the questions which the audit manager must answer to his own satisfaction can only be dealt with properly 'in the field'. In fact, it is a fundamental tenet of audit supervision that the audit manager should visit his staff regularly at the audit location. In this way he can better assess the quality of their work by means of sample checking, and he can gain first-hand experience of the way his staff conduct themselves and can judge with more certainty the nature of the working relationships that have been established.

Most auditing is unremarkable and unsung, but nevertheless effective. There is merit in maintaining a quiet presence and in avoiding sensationalism in report or publication of 'successes'. Often the adequacy of audit is best assessed through manifestations of an effective audit presence, in the form of attitudes and reactions to internal audit presence and action. Too often audit is judged on the basis of exceptions – frauds not detected and irregularities missed. Too often auditors go for the safe areas and the easy pickings in the search for power and promotion.

It is the Grays, Poulsons, Crown Agents which are remembered – not the honest endeavour and the quiet assurance. And if you find nothing, have you necessarily failed? Too often the auditor is blamed as a goalkeeper and the critics overlook the lapses of the appointed defenders. One thing is certain – you cannot win.

CHAPTER 11

External audit

Whilst this book has been written largely with internal audit in mind, it would be incomplete without some reference to the role and the activities of the external auditor. Much of what has been said throughout this book applies equally to external and internal auditors and the differences relate more to emphasis than to objectives. An external auditor who reads Chapter 1 on role and objectives of internal audit would find little with which to disagree in regard to his own sphere of responsibility. The differences, such as they are, would relate to perspective, accountability, independence and emphasis.

Perspective of external audit

'Perspective' is mentioned because external audit is an independent appraisal function *outwith* an organisation. This obviously adds to independence but has the disadvantage of divorcing the auditor from the internal system of communication and information. Internal auditors who have transferred to external audit often comment that, previously, they knew where the skeletons were but did not have the power to act – now they have the power but do not know where to find the skeletons. However, this wider perspective allows the external auditor to view the organisation from a more detached and impersonal stance, and, as his wider remit covers other organisations, this facilitates comparisons and allows the percolation of ideas between organisations.

Accountability

Obviously the external auditor has different lines of accountability from the internal auditor. An internal auditor is primarily responsible to management, although he also owes a duty to the 'client' – i.e. the ratepayer, taxpayer, consumer, etc. However, the external auditor is primarily responsible to the 'client', and his responsibility to management could be said to be secondary. Thus, for example, in the case of local authorities, the external auditor works on behalf of the ratepayers/taxpayers, to ensure that the money they provide is spent wisely on the statutory functions of the authority and is properly accounted for.

Appointment of auditors and its effect on independence

The additional independence of the external auditor has been mentioned earlier. In certain cases this is eroded, to some extent, by the method by which he is selected and this varies considerably between types of public sector organisation. However professional he may be, an external auditor who is directly appointed by the body he audits, and who holds his appointment at its pleasure, is more likely to dilute his criticisms of that body than if he had been appointed independently. Despite this indisputable fact, many public sector organisations continue to be allowed to appoint their own auditors. Even in English and Welsh local authorities, where the previous practice of appointing their own auditors has recently changed, the Audit Commission is still required to consult with the authorities before an appointment is made. In the Scottish local authority system, however, external auditors are appointed by an independent body (the Accounts Commission) without any requirement to consult. In the public corporations such as British Rail, the National Coal Board, the British Gas Corporation, etc., the appointments are generally made by the Secretary of State.

Operational emphasis

The operational emphasis of internal and external audit is different. The internal auditor concentrates his attention upon internal controls within the organisation, with a view to ensuring the security of assets, the reliability of records, economy, efficiency, effectiveness and adherence to policy. Whilst the external auditor is interested in each of these areas and, indeed, devotes a good part of his audit to them, he is also anxious to ensure that the organisation acts only within its statutory powers and that the accounts of the organisation present a fair picture of its activities.

Powers

The powers of external auditors, unlike those of internal auditors, which are internally delegated, generally stem from statute. Thus, for example, an external auditor to a local authority will have his broad responsibilities and powers defined by a series of Acts of Parliament. However, these will generally be extended and amplified in a variety of ways; for example, by standards and guidelines issued by employing organisations (e.g. the Audit Commission) and professional bodies. Generally speaking, these are extended responsibilities, rather than powers.

Planning and control

The planning and control of external audit work follows the same principles as many of internal audit. The major differences being geographical complications – it will be more difficult to arrange an audit of the Orkney Islands Council than of the local polytechnic – and the variety and range of audits undertaken. Techniques differ very little and, indeed, the external auditor will often place much reliance upon the tests carried out by internal audit.

Reporting lines

The greatest difference between internal and external audit lies, perhaps, in the field of audit reporting. This stems largely from the 'accountability' factor mentioned earlier. The internal auditor is mainly responsible to management and it is largely to management that he reports. Whilst the external auditor will also report to management (how else could they be expected to take remedial action?), he will generally also have an external reporting function. This varies considerably between types of organisation so that, for example, an external auditor to a Scottish local authority reports to the authority and, simultaneously, to the Controller of Audit. The Controller of Audit then has a statutory duty to report to the Accounts Commission if he is of the opinion that an item of account is contrary to law, that there has been a failure to bring a sum into account or to carry out a statutory duty, that there has been a loss due to negligence or misconduct, or that incorrect accounting has been done. However, his counterpart in England and Wales would not report to the Controller of Audit if he were of the opinion that an item of account was unlawful; instead, he would go directly to the Courts.

At the end of the audit, an external auditor is required to provide a certificate for the accounts. Depending upon the results of the audit, this may be a 'qualified' or an 'unqualified' certificate. Where an auditor provides an 'unqualified' certificate it does not necessarily mean that he has found nothing amiss. It merely means that he is satisfied that those items he has found do not materially affect the picture presented by the accounts and there is nothing which he feels that he needs to draw to the public's attention. Generally his certificate will be accompanied by a report to management, drawing attention to those matters which require its attention but which do not merit inclusion as a 'qualification' to his certificate.

Quality control

If press reports are to be believed, there is a growing dissatisfaction with external auditors amongst private sector organisations. The whole question of the value received from the audit fee seems to be the subject of debate. Perhaps this dissatisfaction stems from a lack of any independent quality control system. Certainly firms of accountants operate internal peer reviews and some of the more progressive have even introduced reciprocal peer reviews between themselves. However, this does not really satisfy the undoubted need for a really independent form of quality control. However, in the public sector, much stricter systems of quality control exist. Just as external auditors have a duty to review the quality of internal audit, it is generally the case that some form of independent quality review of the external audit function exists. In the case of local authority external auditors, this is carried out by the Audit Commission in England and Wales, and by the Accounts Commission in Scotland. An example of the type of check list used in such quality reviews has been given in Appendix 4 and this demonstrates the range and depth of the exercise.

Privatisation of internal audit

It will be useful to discuss the issue of 'privatisation' of internal audit here. Some public sector organisations seek to use firms of private accountants to carry out their internal audit function on a project basis. Usually this is where there is a temporary additional workload, or where the authority requires its internal audit staff to concentrate on non-audit work on a temporary basis. There have been cases, however, where the solution to the non-existence of an internal audit function has been to appoint a firm of accountants. It is the authors' considered view that an external firm of accountants, however competent they may be, cannot adequately take on the role of internal audit. Internal audit, to state the obvious, should be internal to the organisation; it should have a firmly established tap root into the communication systems (official and unofficial) of the organisation and it should carry out a 'continuous appraisal function' (see the 'role and objectives statement' on page 94). A firm of external accountants cannot meet these criteria in an adequate fashion.

National Audit Office

Finally, no chapter on public sector external audit would be complete without some mention of the National Audit Office. Arising from a growing demand for greater public and parliamentary accountability, the Committee of Public Accounts conducted an inquiry and recommended certain changes in the functions of the Comptroller and Auditor General (the Head of the Exchequer and Audit Department). Many of these recommendations were enacted in the National Audit Act 1983 which strengthened the Comptroller and Auditor General's independence from the executive and created a closer relationship with Parliament.

The National Audit Office was created with the Comptroller and Auditor General as its chief executive. His access to public bodies was clarified and statutory authority was provided for his value-for-money work. He is required to audit the appropriation, revenue, trading and store accounts of all government departments, including other accounts specified by the Exchequer and by audit department acts and statutes, and must report as necessary to Parliament on matters arising from the audits. He has the right of access to other bodies for which he is not the auditor, but which are largely financed from public funds (this excludes nationalised industries and local authorities). Finally, he carries out value-for-money investigations for those bodies for whom he is the appointed auditor, or where he has rights of access, and reports to Parliament on the outcome.

CHAPTER 12

National developments

In Chapter 2, the impact of standards on auditing was discussed and the publication of three sets of internal audit standards in the last five years was referred to. There have been so many other significant developments at national level that it is important to include a brief résumé on the current state of play. Unfortunately, it is a developing situation and it follows that the authors can only reflect the position at the time of writing. The book will be subject to review, but some of the developments occur fairly rapidly and it may be necessary to ascertain the precise situation from time to time from journals such as *Public Finance and Accountancy*.

The Auditing Practices Committee of the Consultative Committee of Accountancy Bodies

Background

The Auditing Practices Committee (APC) was established as a Committee of the Consultative Committee of Accountancy Bodies (CCAB) in 1976 to advance standards of auditing in the profession. It has chosen to effect this by issuing guidance on the best auditing practice on a number of levels, which, in order of status, are as follows:

1. Auditing standards.
2. Auditing guidelines.
3. Audit briefs.
4. True and fair bulletins.

The first of its auditing standards and guidelines, published in April 1980, was mainly a codification of existing best practice. Although addressed primarily to professional auditors in the private sector, the guidance contains much of equal relevance in the public sector.

In October 1982, the Chartered Institute of Public Finance and Accountancy (CIPFA) became a full governing member of the APC. In the following December, the APC decided to include topics in its work plan which were of special relevance to the public sector. Resources have now been made available to bring those plans to fruition. The initiative is well timed as it arises in a period of rapid change and reappraisal in public sector auditing during which the following happened:

1. The Exchequer and Audit Department was developed into the National Audit Office, and the Audit Commission for Local Authorities in England and Wales was established.
2. The involvement of the professional firms in the audit of public sector bodies grew rapidly.
3. There was an upsurge in internal audit activity in central government.
4. The Government mounted a Financial Management Initiative.
5. The statutory powers of value-for-money auditing were granted to the National Audit Office, the Audit Commission and the External Auditors of Water Authorities.

The APC's role in the public sector

Determination of what constitutes best auditing practice is to a large extent dependent upon access to the broadest possible spread of experience. The APC, through the collective membership of its governing bodies, taps expertise from all sectors of commerce, industry and the public domain. Its published guidance is intended to advance standards of auditing as a discipline of universal application. Wherever practicable and applicable, the APC incorporates in its guidance the principles underpinning the statements and guidelines of the Union Européenne des Experts Comptables (UEC) and the International Federation of Accountants (IFAC). By participating in the work of the APC and adopting its guidance where appropriate, the public sector is both contributing to, and benefiting from, auditing experience and expertise worldwide. It also assists the establishment of a common basis of understanding between accountants and auditors in the public and private sectors – an important factor now that private firms audit a significant proportion of public sector bodies.

Public sector initiative

The APC has created its public sector initiative to ensure that public sector considerations are taken into account as appropriate in the preparation of all APC guidance. In addition, the APC is considering the feasibility of producing guidance on topics of particular relevance to the public sector. Several likely subjects have already been identified, as follows:

1. The conduct of value-for-money work.
2. The audit implications of a high level of regulation.
3. The auditor's responsibilities in the public sector in relation to fraud and corrupt practices, given the high standard of probity and accountability demanded of those dealing with public funds.
4. The special role of internal audit in the public sector.
5. The effects of special standards of accountability and integrity on concepts such as materiality and due professional care.
6. The profit motive as a hidden element of control and the need, in its absence, for other formal controls (or audit assessment tools) such as performance indicators.

The APC will examine these topics in the order of priority set out above, although additional subjects of concern to auditors in the public sector may be dealt with as the need arises.

Review of the relevance to the public sector of existing APC guidance

Auditing standards in the public sector are, in most cases, primarily the responsibility of the statutory audit bodies in the various areas concerned. The National Audit Office, the Audit Commission for Local Authorities in England and Wales, the Accounts Commission for Scotland, and the Department of Health and Social Security have all assumed responsibility for setting the standards for external audit of bodies falling within their responsibility. The powers of the Audit Commission have been given statutory authority. The Treasury sets standards for, and issues guidelines on the practice to be applied to, the internal audit of government departments and public bodies sponsored by those departments. The CCAB, the APC and individual professional accountancy bodies recognise and accept this position.

Statutory public sector audit bodies cannot cede their responsibilities to the APC. Nevertheless, each of the bodies recognises the APC guidance as a reflection of best practice. It is desirable that, by virtue of the initiative, such bodies should choose to adopt APC standards and guidelines as general guidance, and elaborate with their own detailed guidance as necessary.

APC guidance

As mentioned earlier, four types of document are issued. The most authoritative are *auditing standards* and *auditing guidelines*. They are supplemented by *audit briefs* and by *true and fair bulletins* which are issued three times a year.

AUDITING STANDARDS

These prescribe the basic principles and practices which members of the accountancy bodies (and other organisations which adopt the standards) are expected to follow in the conduct of an audit. Unless otherwise indicated in the text, auditing standards apply whenever an audit is carried out.

AUDITING GUIDELINES

Auditing guidelines are not mandatory, but members of accountancy bodies have been advised that a court of law may, when considering the adequacy of the work of an auditor, take into account the pronouncement or publications which it considers may be indicative of good practice. Auditing standards and guidelines are likely to be so regarded. The guidelines give guidance on the following:

1. The procedures by which auditing standards may be applied.
2. The application of auditing standards to specific items which appear in financial statements.
3. The audit problems which relate to particular industries and service organisations.

AUDIT BRIEFS

These booklets do not have the authority of auditing standards and guidelines, and are published by the APC to meet a number of different purposes. These have included the following:

1. Raising controversial issues.
2. Giving an explanation to users on what is an audit.
3. Issuing guidance on the audit implications of recent legislation.
4. Issuing practical guidance which is too detailed to be included in an auditing guideline.

TRUE AND FAIR BULLETINS

The APC publishes this bulletin to advise members of matters which concern auditors, and to give information on what the APC is currently doing. Normally, the articles included in the bulletin reflect the views of the individual authors.

Applicability of auditing standards

The APC has published a matrix of present and prospective standards and guidelines (see Fig. 3). Four standards have been proposed to date, of which three have been published; the fourth is currently being drafted. The published standards are reviewed below.

THE AUDITOR'S OPERATIONAL STANDARD

This states that the auditor should do the following:

1. He should adequately plan, control and record his work.
2. He should ascertain the system of recording and processing transactions and assess its adequacy as a basis for the preparation of financial statements.
3. He should obtain relevant and reliable evidence sufficient to enable him to draw reasonable conclusions therefrom.
4. Where he wishes to place reliance on any internal controls, he should ascertain and evaluate them and perform compliance tests on their operation.
5. He should carry out such a review of the financial statements as is sufficient in conjunction with the conclusions drawn from other audit evidence obtained, to give him a reasonable basis for his opinion on the financial statements.

Where the auditor has followed the operational standard and such of the other three standards as are applicable, it follows that he can state in his report on the financial statements involved that he has 'audited in accordance with approved auditing standards'. This would be so, even in the case of certain public sector audits, for example, where, because the auditor does not report in 'true and fair' terms, or his report conveys added meaning to similar wording as used in the private sector, the other three standards would not apply.

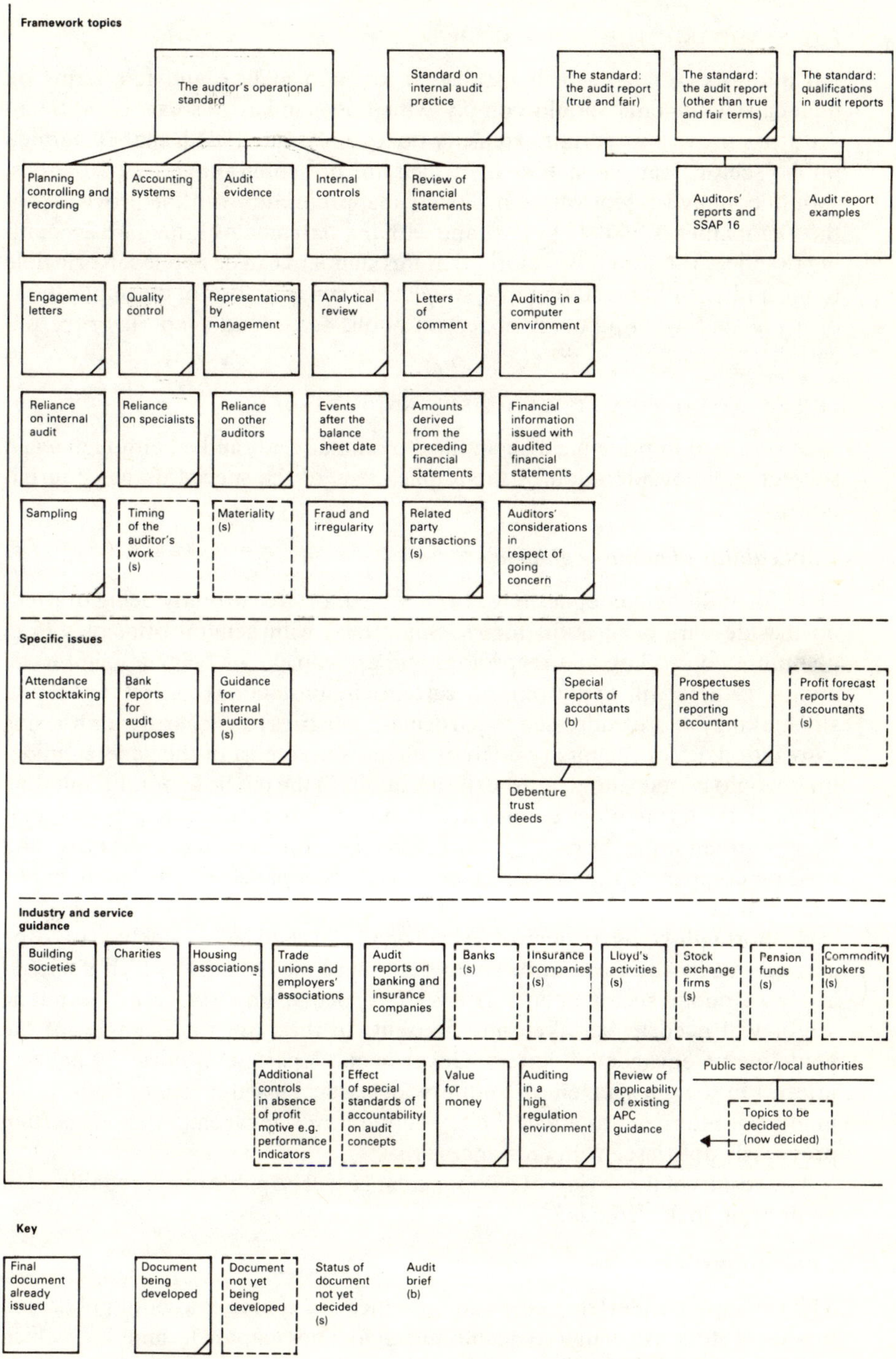

Fig. 3 *Matrix of present and prospective auditing standards and guidelines.*

THE STANDARD: THE AUDIT REPORT

All auditors' reports which express an opinion in true and fair terms on financial statements should comply with this standard insofar as pertinent statutory provisions permit. Treasury policy since July 1983 is that all audited public sector financial statements which are presented on an accruals basis, should comply (except where positively inappropriate) with the provisions of the Companies Acts 1948 to 1981 and with the statements of standard accounting practice. It follows, therefore, that this standard can be applied in principle to the audit of all such statements, subject to a consideration of the implications of using special terminology in certain public sector audit reports or 'certificates'.

THE STANDARD: QUALIFICATIONS IN AUDIT REPORTS

This standard in principle also applies to public sector audits, although again subject to a consideration of the implications of the special usage of terminology.

Applicability of auditing guidelines

Over 30 auditing guidelines have been issued, or are currently being drafted, on a wide variety of audit topics. Some deal with general principles (e.g. planning, controlling and recording) and are capable of being applied to all audits. Others will apply only in certain circumstances (e.g. attendance at stocktaking) or are addressed to particular industries (e.g. charities or housing associations). A preliminary analysis suggests that most of the general guidelines would be relevant to most external audits in the public sector. Frequently, although the terminology employed in them refers particularly to private sector bodies or auditing firms (e.g. directors, general meeting, enterprise and holding company), the principles involved can apply equally to many public sector audits.

A thorough-going review of every APC standard and guideline is to be carried out by the APC in order to determine the extent to which it should apply to public sector audits. Issues of particular importance in the public sector will need to be taken into account. In the case, for example, of the guideline on engagement letters, Government departments normally have an interest in the engagement of auditors for particular public sector bodies, but might not intervene to affect the terms of a firm's engagement unless certain previously unforeseen circumstances arise.

The results of the review of extant guidance will be published, probably as an audit brief, in due course.

Conclusions

The principles underlying best audit practice are common to both public and private sectors. Although some auditing guidelines employ terminology which is used most frequently in private sector organisations and audits, their guidance is generally capable of a much wider application. The APC public sector initiative provides an opportunity for such guidance to be translated into public sector terms, and for public sector requirements to be identified at the formative stage of all future standards and guidelines. It is to be hoped that bodies responsible for setting auditing standards in public sector bodies will participate fully in doing the following:

1. Identifying issues to be taken into account in the issue of further APC guidance.
2. Providing representation for working parties preparing guidance on particular public sector topics.
3. Adopting APC guidance, wherever relevant, as an indication of best practice to be followed in the conduct of all public sector audits.

APPENDIX 1

CIPFA statements on internal audit practice in the public sector

Contents

Published by:
THE CHARTERED INSTITUTE OF PUBLIC FINANCE AND ACCOUNTANCY,
1 Buckingham Place, London SW1E 6HS. Tel: 01-828 7661.

1

Preface

The Statements were prepared by a sub-group of the Institute's Audit Panel which was formed in 1975.

The members of the sub-group are:

J B G Bell (Chairman)	— Middlesbrough B C
R Burns	— Strathclyde R C
P A Dowsett	— G L C
M J Dymond (Vice Chairman)	— Government Accountancy Service
J Elwin	— Greater Manchester P T E
D Gadbury	— Southern Water Authority
P W Heppleston	— District Audit Service
P Kimmance	— District Audit Service
B O'Riordan	— Essex C C
G Potter (Secretary)	— C I P F A

Acknowledgement is also due to:

B C Cranwell (Chairman of Panel)	— Nottinghamshire C C
R Buttery (Vice Chairman of Panel)	— Lincolnshire C C
B Marsden	— Coventry M B C

for their assistance in the final stages of the work.

Further copies of the Statements are available from the Institute Director

2

Introduction

Purpose

The Chartered Institute of Public Finance and Accountancy is publishing the 'Statements on Internal Audit Practice in the Public Sector' in recognition of the need to promote the establishment of high professional standards of internal audit practice throughout the public sector.

Scope

At present there are no published statements for internal audit in the public sector and existing practice is based on a variety of guidelines which come from a number of sources. By compiling statements for auditors and those responsible for the internal audit function, it has been possible to codify the basic factors contained in existing material to form one source against which future performance can be judged. It is, therefore, recognised that some authorities may well be operating the internal audit function in accordance with some, or all, of the Statements. However, for the first time, the operation and conduct of the internal audit function in the public sector has been set down for the use of all authorities. The principles enunciated in the Statements are intended to apply to all internal audits conducted by public sector organisations irrespective of their size.

The Statements prescribe basic principles and practices which should be followed in the conduct of all internal audits where the auditor is called upon to express an opinion upon the soundness, adequacy and application of internal control and to report independently thereon. The Statements are not presented as a definitive code capable of meeting all circumstances as this would necessarily suppress developments in internal auditing.

The Statements have been prepared for the guidance of directors of finance, chief internal auditors, and those whose responsibility it is to provide an internal audit service within the public sector. For this purpose the term 'public sector'includes local authorities, public boards, and government departments.

Although the Statements are not issued as an enforceable code, the Institute Council recommends their adoption by directors of finance and chief internal auditors.

Classification

The Statements have been classified under two main headings:

- **i)** General—pertaining to auditing philosophy and principles,
- **ii)** Operational—embracing matters directly concerned with internal audit practice, covering scope of audit, audit management, reporting and relationships.

Each Statement is divided into two parts:

- **i)** The Statement—defining the prime objectives,
- **ii)** An Explanation giving guidance on its application.

Glossary of Terms

A glossary of terms used is provided and unless otherwise stated, the term 'auditor' refers to the internal auditor.

Bernard Cranwell
Chairman, Audit Panel

3

Role and Objectives Statement

Internal Audit:
is an independent appraisal function within an organisation, for the review of activities as a service to all levels of management. It is a control which measures, evaluates and reports upon the effectiveness of internal controls, financial and other, as a contribution to the efficient use of resources within an organisation.

Internal Control
Management has the responsibility to establish internal control so that its activities are conducted in an efficient and well ordered manner. Internal control comprises the whole system of controls and methods, both financial and otherwise, which are established by management to:

- **i)** safeguard its assets;
- **ii)** ensure reliability of records;
- **iii)** promote operational efficiency; and
- **iv)** monitor adherence to policies and directives.

Responsibility of Internal Audit
It is the responsibility of internal audit to review, appraise and report upon:

- **a)** The soundness, adequacy and application of internal controls;
- **b)** The extent to which thc organisation's assets and interests are accounted for and safeguarded from losses of all kinds arising from:
  - **i)** fraud and other offences
  - **ii)** waste, extravagance and inefficient administration, poor value for money or other cause.
- **c)** The suitability and reliability of financial and other management data developed within the organisation.

Independence
For internal audit to fulfil these responsibilities it is essential that it operates with independence, obtained primarily through adequate scope, authority and objectivity:

Co-operation
Other Departments:
The independent role of internal audit should in no way diminish the close working relationship with other departments of an organisation through contact at the appropriate managerial levels before, during and at the conclusion of audit assignments.

External Audit:
There should be co-operation between internal audit and external audit, which is statutorily appointed, including the exchange of relevant information in order to maximise audit resources.

4

Summary of Statements

Independence
Internal audit must be sufficiently independent to enable the auditor to perform his duties in a manner which will allow his professional judgements and recommendations to be effective and impartial.

Due Professional Care
The internal auditor shall exercise due professional care in carrying out his duties.

Internal Control
Internal audit shall review the soundness, adequacy and application of internal controls both financial and otherwise.

Irregularities and Fraud
The internal auditor shall endeavour to reveal any serious defect in systems of internal control which might lead to the perpetration of irregularities and fraud and must have regard to the possibility of malpractice in areas under examination. He shall be alert to the possibility of corruption and be prepared to inform the appropriate level of management of any justifiable suspicions.

Planning and Control
Internal audit work must be planned and controlled in order to achieve the agreed objectives of the internal audit department, to establish audit priorities and to ensure the effective use of audit resources.

Supervision
Supervision during the preparation, conduct and closure of an internal audit is fundamental to effective audit practice.

Training
An internal auditor must be properly trained to fulfil his responsibilities.

Evidence
The internal auditor must have adequate and relevant evidence on which to base his conclusions and recommendations.

Reporting
The findings and recommendations arising from an internal audit must be promptly conveyed to management.

External Audit
The relationship with the external auditor should be based on an understanding of his role and on a degree of co-operation including the exchange of relevant information sufficient to maximise audit performance.

Client Departments
The relationship between the internal auditor and the management and staff of the departments subject to audit must be based on mutual confidence and understanding.

Other Review Agencies
The internal auditor's relationship with other review agencies must be based on mutual confidence and understanding but must not compromise the relationship between the auditor and client departments.

5

General Statements

The Statements included in this section are concerned primarily with those aspects which are of general concern to the internal auditor.

INDEPENDENCE

STATEMENT

Internal audit must be sufficiently independent to enable the auditor to perform his duties in a manner which will allow his professional judgements and recommendations to be effective and impartial.

EXPLANATION

Role of Internal Audit

The CIPFA 'Statement on the Role and Objectives of Internal Audit in the Public Sector' defines the need for independence. In particular it deals with the scope authority and objectivity of internal audit. The role of internal audit depends upon formal recognition by the highest levels of management of the value of the independence of the internal audit function.

Organisation of Internal Audit

The principle elements of independence which should be present for internal audit to operate effectively are:

1. Internal audit should have direct access to all departmental heads, the chief executive and/or the management board.
2. Internal audit should be independent of personnel directly responsible for the operations under review.
3. Internal audit should be completely independent of all financial systems operating within the organisation. Involvement in routine departmental procedures will inevitably impair the work of the audit department.
4. The chief internal auditor should have the right of reporting without editing under his own name.
5. The chief internal auditor should have the right of reporting on any aspect of the financial work including that of the finance department.

Operation of Internal Audit

Internal audit activity should be unrestricted and auditors should have full rights of access to records, assets and personnel and should receive such information and explanations as they consider necessary for the performance of their duties.

Internal audit should be informed and consulted about any proposed changes in systems of internal control and may make recommendations on the standards of control to be applied in the development of systems and procedures under review. For example, advice should be given on the controls to be incorporated in new or revised systems before implementation. This should not prejudice internal audit's objectivity in reviewing that system.

Internal audit should not be directly responsible for the development or implementation of new systems, or engage in any other activity which they would normally review and appraise since this could compromise their independence.

Independence of the Internal Auditor

If the auditor cannot, for any reason, produce unbiased judgements, opinions, and recommendations, then he should declare his position prominently in the audit report.

The auditor should have an objective attitude of mind and be in a sufficiently independent position to enable him to exercise his judgements, express his opinions and present his recommendations with impartiality.

The following are examples of the circumstances which may impair the auditor's independence:

1. Professional or personal relationships the nature of which might cause the auditor to limit the extent or character of his audit.
2. Previous involvement in a decision-making or management capacity in the operations under audit.
3. Any pecuniary interest, direct or indirect, in an organisation or activity which is subject to audit.
4. Any internal/external influences which seek to restrict or modify the scope or conduct of the audit.
5. Any means employed to overrule or significantly influence the auditor's judgement as to the content of the audit report.

DUE PROFESSIONAL CARE

STATEMENT

The auditor shall exercise due professional care in carrying out his duties.

EXPLANATION

The Internal Auditor's Responsibilities

The auditor's responsibilities are not unlimited. He is required to carry out audits with reasonable skill. The case law quoted in the footnote relates specifically to external auditors but it is considered that the judgements give some guidance as to the level of performance required of the internal auditor.

Due professional care may therefore be defined as the application of that measure of skill and care which might reasonably be expected of a competent auditor relative to the specific duties undertaken.

Due professional care does not demand infallibility of the auditor, but only that reasonable care and competence is exercised. He must conduct his examination by making those tests and checks which, in the exercise of his judgement and skill, he considers necessary for the particular audit.

7

Level of Performance
In order to demonstrate that he has exercised due professional care, the auditor must be able to show that in his work he has reached an acceptable level of performance as illustrated by these Statements. This requires him to ensure in particular that:

1. Audits are properly planned;
2. Audits are supervised and performed by auditors of appropriate experience;
3. That relevant tests are devised and properly applied in sufficient depth; and
4. Conclusions are soundly based on relevant and properly documented facts.

Quality of Performance
The quality of an audit depends to a large extent on the exercise of proper judgement by an auditor in planning audit work and choosing audit tests. In order to do this, he must:

1. Have a satisfactory understanding of relevant law, recommendations made by professional accountancy bodies and internal financial regulations;
2. Know the aims of the organisation under audit, the way in which it is structured, its system of internal control, and what management information is provided;
3. Be aware particularly of unit costs and other measures produced both internally and externally which would enable him to form a view as to the level of performance in the organisation.

Maintenance of Standards
In addition to normal day to day supervision of internal audit work, formal reviews of performance, carried out by senior udit staff or by other experienced auditors will promote a high level of achievement (see Statement on Planning and Control).

Maintenance of the standard of due professional care in the internal audit department's work is the responsibility of the chief internal auditor. In order to ensure a high level of achievement, he must be assisted by sufficient staff both in quality and numbers.

Footnote
'It is the duty of an auditor to bring to bear on the work he has to perform that skill, care, and caution which a reasonably competent, careful, and cautious auditor would use. What is reasonable skill, care and caution must depend on the particular circumstances of each case . . . If there is anything calculated to excite suspicion he should probe it to the bottom; but in the absence of anything of that kind, he is only bound to be reasonably cautious and careful . . . The duties of auditors must not be rendered too onerous . . .' (In re Kingston Cotton Mill Co Ltd., (1896) 2 Ch 279). This definition has been approved in more recent judgements, although it would be as well to bear in mind Mr. Justice Pennycuick's words delivered in his judgement, In re Thomas Gerrard & Co Ltd., (1967) Ch D 522: '. . . the standards of reasonable care and skill are, on expert evidence, more exacting today than those which prevailed in 1896 . . . '.

Operational Statements

The Statements included in this section refer to those aspects which are concerned with the manner in which the internal auditor carries out his duties.

The Statements are presented under four main headings:

Scope of Internal Audit
Internal Audit Management
Internal Audit Reporting
Internal Audit Relationships

Scope of Internal Audit

The Statements in this section are concerned with the scope of activity of the internal audit function.

INTERNAL CONTROL

STATEMENT

Internal audit shall review the soundness, adequacy and application of internal controls both financial and otherwise.

EXPLANATION

Definition of Internal Control

Internal control has been defined in the Role and Objectives Statement as comprising the whole system of controls and methods both financial and otherwise, which are established by management to:

1 Safeguard its assets;
2 Ensure reliability of records;
3 Promote operational efficiency; and
4 Monitor adherence to policies and directives.

Internal controls can be divided into two main categories: financial controls, which are primarily concerned with the legitimacy of expenditure and the security of assets and income; and other controls, which are created and maintained by management to ensure that an activity is relevant to the needs of an organisation and is carried out in the most effective manner. These categories are interdependent, and should not be regarded in isolation as both have an impact on the performance of activities and their consequent cost and value to the organisation.

The main areas of internal control can be more closely defined as follows:

Financial Control

i) Budgetary Control: The organisation should plan and control its expenditure and income to meet its predetermined objectives.

ii) Legitimacy of Income and Expenditure: All income and expenditure should be in accordance with the policies of the organisation, should be properly authorised and should be within the law.

iii) Security of Assets: Assets of the organisation should be kept in proper custody and not wrongly applied, either by error or intent.

iv) Accounting Controls: All transactions should be correctly recorded and accurately processed, and control accounts maintained.

Management Control

The nature of management controls will vary widely according to the type of activity which is under review. However, there are several basic control areas which should always be in evidence:

i) Objectives: The organisation should regularly review its objectives relating to any operational activity and determine the methods needed to achieve them. Management has the responsibility for determining objectives, policies and plans, and the auditor should not intervene in such processes. An audit may show inadequate controls on the supply of information to management for decision making. These aspects are legitimate areas of audit concern, and may well require comments on the correctness of the decisions themselves, but the auditor should be wary of basing comments purely on the advantages given him by hindsight.

ii) Procedures: Staff at all levels need to be regularly informed both of their overall objectives and the organisational procedures which are to be followed in order to ensure the achievement of the operational activity.

iii) Organisation: The organisational structure should be clearly defined and adequate to ensure that staff appreciate their role, responsibilities and obligations.

iv) Management Information: Management needs to be continually informed, with relevant and up-to-date data, of the financial and operational performance of any activity under its control.

v) Supervision: Systems of supervision and internal check (eg division of duties, independent checking of work, quality control etc.) should be maintained to ensure that breakdowns, including irregularities and fraud, or weaknesses within the operation are revealed at an early stage.

vi) Reviews of Operational Effectiveness: Management should regularly review the effectiveness and efficiency of operations under its control, and consider their continued relevance in the light of changing circumstances.

Economic Use of Resources

Primarily the responsibility of internal audit is to examine systems of control. Nevertheless, the auditor should look beyond controls to the relationship of expenditure to the objectives of the organisation, eg cost effectiveness, utilisation of resources.

Audit Approach

The objective of the auditor's examination of the system is to arrive at an opinion which can form the basis of a constructive report to management. In conducting the examination the auditor should:

1 Identify the purpose of the operation/activity under review.

2 Ascertain, record and test the system of internal control.

3 Assess the system for its strengths and weaknesses.

10

4 Evaluate the possible effects of any shortcomings or deviations.
5 Report.

In some areas management may regard the operation of an adequate system of internal control as impracticable considering the costs which would be involved and the benefits which would be achieved. In such circumstances the role of audit is to ascertain whether such a decision appears to be justified and to assess whether management has instituted acceptable procedures which minimise, as far as possible, the risk of errors, omissions, waste or fraud. The auditor will then form an opinion, based on detailed checking and validation, whether the account or activity may be relied upon. In extreme cases it may be appropriate for the auditor to categorise such situations as unauditable and to report accordingly.

IRREGULARITIES AND FRAUD

STATEMENT

The internal auditor shall endeavour to reveal any serious defect in systems of internal control which might lead to the perpetration of fraud and must have regard to the possibility of malpractice in areas under examination. He shall be alert to the possibility of corruption and be prepared to inform the appropriate level of management of any justifiable suspicions.

EXPLANATION

The Internal Auditor's Role

Prevention and detection of irregularities and fraud are only part of the auditor's duty 'to ensure wise and prudent administration' (Roberts v Hopwood & Others (1925) AC 578). This view is reflected in the Institute's Statement on the Role and Objectives of Internal Audit. It is unrealistic to expect the auditor to detect all losses (arising either from fraud or other causes). (See also Statement on Internal Control.)

The auditor's attitude to the prevention and detection of irregularities and fraud should be that he takes nothing for granted in the matters he is examining. He should identify systems where too much trust has been placed, by design or accident, in one person and transactions where there is an inherently high risk.

A careful assessment of systems should alert the auditor to such vulnerable areas and reveal the possibility of consistent irregularities and fraud.

Although the auditor will recommend, where appropriate, the adoption of procedures which make irregularities and fraud more difficult (eg by the separation and/or rotation of duties) he should be aware that dishonest persons acting in collusion can defeat any normal system. He should also note that irregularities and fraud of a collusive nature usually came to light not directly as a result of audit work but indirectly from information volunteered by persons within or outside the organisation under audit. If the auditor is seen to be readily accessible it is likely that information of this nature will come his way particularly if it is known that such information will be treated in confidence as far as it is possible to do so.

Corruption will not normally be detected in any examination of accounts. The auditor should ensure that any suspicion of corruption is investigated to the best of his ability.

11

When aware of possible irregularity or fraud the auditor may be tempted to keep his suspicions to himself until he has obtained conclusive proof. However, others may have additional information which would resolve the matter and, once he has *prima facie* evidence, the auditor must take action in accordance with the procedures laid down by management.

The auditor should make careful preparations for interviewing persons in cases where irregularity or fraud may be suspected. The originals of all documents under question must be impounded and a check list prepared of points to be covered. A reliable witness should be available at such interviews and a careful note, signed by the auditor and witness, should be made of proceedings. (See Statement on Evidence).

The stage at which the police should be informed depends on local practice but the auditor should be careful to avoid taking over the role of the police or compromising subsequent police investigations if there is the possibility that a criminal offence may be involved.

The subseqent discovery of irregularities and fraud in an area which has already been examined by the auditor is not in itself evidence of inadequate performance on his part, unless the irregularity or fraud is so consistent or blatant that proper audit tests and enquiries should have brought it to notice.

Internal Audit Management

The Statements in this section are concerned with the management of the internal audit function.

PLANNING AND CONTROL

STATEMENT

Internal audit work must be planned and controlled in order to achieve the agreed objectives of the internal audit department, to establish audit priorities and to ensure the effective use of audit resources.

EXPLANATION

The elements of any operational cycle are planning, implementation, control and review.

Planning

Planning is concerned with defining objectives, setting priorities and the subsequent allocation of resources over a period of time.

It is necessary:

1 To define the field of audit activity by clearly setting out the objective of each audit area,
  - i) character (eg the relative emphasis upon protection, value for money or cost effectiveness); and,
  - ii) confidence levels required (eg extent, frequency, depth, degree of risk).

2 To identify the resources needed and reconcile to the resources available.

3 To determine the time period of the audit plan.

4 To co-ordinate the audit plan with that prepared by the external auditors. (See Statement on External Audit).

Within the overall objectives of the audit department, there will be a need to change emphasis from time to time. This might be indicated by changes within services, departmental reorganisation, system change or simply a domestic decision to concentrate on a specific topic or aspect. The plan must be sufficiently flexible to allow a prompt response to unscheduled audit work, eg special investigations or specific allegations of fraud.

The audit resources needed to meet the agreed objectives should be measured as accurately as possible. Where existing resources are inadequate the director of finance or management board will have to decide after discussion with the chief auditor whether additional resources should be provided or the objectives modified to reflect agreed audit priorities.

The time element is an inseparable part of the audit plan, which may be divided into three parts as follows:

i) Long term or strategic plan, providing a framework within which the internal audit department will operate. It should set out the audit objectives in broad terms, the areas to be covered, and the frequency of coverage reconciled with the resources allocated. It should cover a period of the order of two to five years and should be subject to review on an annual basis. It should be a general target setting exercise, rather than a detailed resource allocating exercise, although resources must be taken into account.

ii) Medium term or tactical plan, which translates the long term plan into a programme of audits to be carried out. It will be concerned with a shorter period of time but certainly no longer than a year. It should define the objectives of the various audits, determine the allocations of audit resources and must be flexible, with an allowance for contingencies.

iii) Short term or operational plan including the pre-plan will be drawn up for each audit as it is arranged. It should be designed to fit within and to achieve the objectives set out in the medium term plan. The audit should be broken down into its component parts covering such matters as time, budgets and staff allocations, the audit procedures to be used and administrative requirements to be met.

Implementation

Successful implementation depends to a large extent on the personal commitment of the staff to the audit objectives set down in the plans. The concepts of audit planning and the inherent importance of target achievement should be conveyed to all levels of audit staff. The success of any plan depends upon discipline, co-operation and commitment. Successful implementation covers in practice:

Progress Control:
The auditor in charge should report his progress regularly to his supervisor. Where audit findings indicate a significant need for priorities to be re-assessed or for more extensive investigations the auditor in charge should discuss with his supervisor what amendments are necessary in the context of the audit plan.

Quality Control:
It is important to ensure that the levels of performance of the auditors are satisfactory. In the context of effective supervision (see Statement on Supervision), this may be achieved by the setting of standards of work of which these Statements form a part, against which performance can be measured, and the assignment of appropriately qualified and experienced staff.

Control and Review

It is important that the outcome of each audit or group of audits be reviewed in terms of the objectives set and the resources allocated, so that the validity of the audit plan is checked and any necessary revisions are made. This analysis can be on a six monthly, quarterly, monthly or even a weekly basis. The impact of such a review is most likely to be on day to day planning but the possibility of its effect on the annual or long term plan should be considered.

The extent of the audit activity in the medium term should be consolidated into a summary or progress report on say a monthly or quarterly basis, which will give a clear picture of the audit cover, plans and the success in meeting the objectives. The chief internal auditor, in consultation with management and in liaison with external audit, can then determine the future emphasis of audit planning.

14

SUPERVISION

STATEMENT

Supervision during the preparation, conduct and closure of an internal audit is fundamental to effective audit practice.

EXPLANATION

Supervision should ensure the observance of the Audit Statements and the use of appropriate audit techniques.

Comparative abilities and needs of auditors will necessarily influence the degree of supervision.

Audit manuals and associated documentation are valuable aids to supervision.

Preparation

It is desirable that auditors are involved in both the planning and control of audit work. The extent to which this happens will depend on the ability of the auditor carrying out the work and the style of management carried out in the audit section.

The supervisor should ensure that individual auditors:

1 Know the objective of the work undertaken;
2 Have a clear understanding of the scope and depth of the work they are carrying out;
3 Understand the methods to be used before carrying out the work;
4 Know the extent to which planned work may be varied.

Supervision During the Audit

Supervision during the audit involves regular monitoring of progress to ensure that:

1 The audit is proceeding within the budgeted time towards the planned objectives and at the required standards;
2 All aspects are covered within the time allocated;
3 Any significant variations considered necessary by the auditor are sanctioned in advance.

Guidance from the supervisor on any difficulties encountered should be readily available.

Completion of Audit

After completion of the audit, the supervisor should:

1 Assess whether the objectives of the audit have been achieved.
2 Satisfy himself that the audit is documented by working papers that support the findings and conclusions and provide necessary data to prepare a satisfactory report.
3 Ensure that a report is prepared on the completion of the audit (see Statement on Reporting).

TRAINING

STATEMENT
An internal auditor must be properly trained to fulfil his responsibilities.

EXPLANATION
Quality of Work
The work of an internal audit department requires varying degrees of skill and the needs of each task must be matched by an appropriate quality of staff. The department should comprise personnel of varying levels in terms of qualifications and experience to ensure that the work is carried out effectively.

Whilst the employing authority has a duty to ensure that an auditor receives appropriate training for his full range of duties, the auditor should personally keep abreast of current developments affecting his sphere of activity.

Needs of the Individual
Training should be tailored to the needs of the individual and in assessing these needs, due account should be taken of:

1. The audit objectives and priorities established by management;
2. The type of audit work to which he is allocated;
3. His previous training, experience and qualifications.

Scope of Training
Training should be a planned and continuing process at all levels and should cover four main areas:

1. Initial training for newly appointed auditors designed to establish them as useful members of the department. Subjects covered should include the role and objectives of internal audit and the basic principles of auditing;
2. Development training in general audit skills, techniques and behavioural aspects to improve the effectiveness of those who have been employed in an audit department for some time;
3. Management training for auditors who have the potential to manage and direct an audit team;
4. Specialist training for those auditors responsible for a particular activity such as computer application or incentive bonus schemes.

There may be auditors from disciplines other than finance but the majority are likely to have a financial background. A formal qualification is desirable but an auditor also requires aptitude, experience and training.

16

Internal Audit Reporting

The Statements in this section are concerned with the manner by which the internal auditor obtains information and reports.

EVIDENCE

STATEMENT

The internal auditor must have adequate and relevant evidence on which to base his conclusions and recommendations.

EXPLANATION

Nature and Sources of Evidence

Evidence consists of written material, observed events and oral statements.

The written material will include accounting records, minutes, correspondence, and certificates from third parties.

The observation of events may be 'recurring' (for example, attendance at stocktaking) or 'non-recurring' (for example, an observation in response to information received). The auditor should record the results of his observation during their course or as soon as possible afterwards.

Verbal statements may be from diverse sources, including members of staff, members of the public and business contacts (for example, suppliers) of the organisation being audited. Such statements as are relevant should be recorded in writing by the auditor as they are received or as soon as possible afterwards. In some cases the statement may be sufficiently important for the auditor to request that it be made in writing; obviously the auditor's judgement will be involved and each case must be treated on its merits.

Objectivity

The auditor should bear in mind that evidence, whatever its nature and source, may form the basis of proceedings to which legal constraints could apply and that Judges Rules and the provisions of the Civil Evidence Act 1968 may be relevant. Obtaining and assessing such evidence is a step to be taken with great care and each organisation should define clearly the limits of the auditor's responsibility in relation to that of other investigatory authorities, particularly the police. Some guidance is given in an Irish case:

> 'The duties of an auditor are to investigate . . . carefully, to approach the matter impartially, to give every person concerned a just and fair opportunity of making his case, and to arrive at his decision in a judicial way.' (The State at the prosecution of Deane and Ealsh v Moran (8 Ir. L.T. 37) 1953).

Basic Requirements of Evidence

The statement requires evidence to be adequate and relevant.

Adequate evidence presupposes:

1 A degree of testing—the extent of which should be determined by the auditor having regard to the circumstances of the particular audit;
2 Validity (that is to say, reliability and soundness) and;
3 Competence in the person or persons obtaining and interpreting the evidence;

17

sufficient for a conclusion to be formed and supported.

Relevant evidence can be defined as data or facts which are significant in arriving at a conclusion. Care must be taken to ensure a correct balance is obtained since the value of evidence is reduced if it is excessive.

Working Papers

All documentary evidence obtained during the course of an audit should be indexed for easy reference and retained safely as part of the working papers. These will also include audit programmes, internal control questionnaires and other working notes.

Signed and dated working papers, prepared and reviewed at varying stages of an assignment, constitute the link between fieldwork and report. They are the justification in case of challenge, and should be retained for a reasonable period.

REPORTING

STATEMENT

The findings and recommendations arising from an internal audit must be promptly conveyed to management.

EXPLANATION

Form of Reporting

To ensure objectivity:

1 The chief internal auditor should have the right of reporting without editing under his own name.

2 The auditor should have an objective attitude of mind and be in a sufficiently independent position to enable him to exercise his judgement, express his opinions and present his recommendations with impartiality.

3 If an auditor cannot for any reason produce unbiased judgements, opinions and recommendations then he should declare this position prominently in the audit report.

An audit should be a logical sequence of enquiries and tests designed to lead to the production of a report to management. As an audit progresses the auditor will clear with line management many of the minor points which have come to notice during his enquiries and tests. Points of significance which remain at the end of the audit should form the basis of the final discussions with management and in due course the substance of the formal written report. Interim reports are necessary where immediate action is required, eg where financial irregularities, fraud or major discrepancies are discovered.

In reporting it is necessary to determine the significance of each point arising from the audit. This requires the exercise of judgement in the light of such factors as:

1 What may be at risk (ie the potential extent of error);

2 The extent of findings as related to the total population;

3 Importance to the overall responsibility of management;

4 Sensitivity, eg policy, personnel or public interest.

Objectives of Audit Reporting

The principle objectives of reporting are:

18

1 To alert management as soon as possible to matters of significance arising from the audit;

2 To persuade management to implement recommendations for changes leading to improvements in the system and its performance;

3 To provide a formal record of points raised by the audit and, where appropriate, agreements reached with management.

In order to achieve these objectives the report must:

a) Be written in language that is easily understood by the recipient;

b) State the scope, purpose and areas of audit undertaken;

c) Be prepared in a manner that allows management to assess its value in the minimum of time;

d) Be based only on relevant facts and information which are documented in working papers;

e) Draw conclusions from the factual information presented;

f) In making recommendations, reflect the materiality of each point and take account of views and practical comments expressed by management during the audit and the final discussions;

g) Indicate whether the system is operating satisfactorily.

The underlying approach is that matters of consequence should be raised formally in writing, but that minor errors and detailed matters for correction which do not indicate a consistent or systematic weakness should be cleared informally with members of staff directly involved.

Detailed reporting procedures should be tailored, within the general terms of this Statement, to the conventions and requirements of the organisation. In particular individual reports may be consolidated into periodic summary reports (eg to an audit committee) and should be linked with the process of reappraisal of the audit plan. (See Statement on Planning and Control).

Matters found during the course of the audit which have already been cleared by management action should nevertheless be included and acknowledged in the report if, but for the action already taken, they would have been reported formally.

Where an audit has not revealed any matters which require formal reporting action a brief report should be issued stating:

1 That the audit has taken place and indicate the accounts or activities covered;

2 That no matters of consequence have been found.

Distribution

It is essential that all final audit reports are issued as soon as possible after the completion of the audit. Any delay will weaken the impact of the report and postpone the chance of rectifying serious areas of deficiency mentioned in the report.

For the audit report to be effective it is essential that it is distributed to the appropriate management staff. The distribution of reports is a matter for the chief internal auditor but the head of department for the account or activity under audit should always receive a copy.

Follow-up Procedures

Formal follow up procedures should cover:

1. Dates by which replies should be received;
2. Hastening action to be taken;
3. Annotation of the audit files to show the recommendations accepted and changes in procedure agreed; and
4. The need for written replies to all reports.

Response of Management

When an audit report does not receive an acceptable response from management, it will be for decision whether it should be pursued at a more senior level. This decision will depend upon the nature and materiality of the findings and recommendations included in the report. Although it must be accepted that the auditor cannot insist that all its recommendations be followed it is however his duty to ensure that the eventual decision on an audit report has been taken deliberately by management, with full understanding of its substance and at a level appropriate to its significance.

Internal Audit Relationships

The Statements in this section are concerned with the relationships between the internal auditor and other parties.

EXTERNAL AUDIT

STATEMENT

The relationship with the external auditor should be based on an understanding of his role and on a degree of co-operation including the exchange of relevant information sufficient to maximise audit performance.

EXPLANATION

Role of External and Internal Audit

Co-operation between external and internal audit needs to take account of their differing roles and responsibilities.

The external auditor has the duty to report as to the accuracy and legality of the accounts and this responsibility cannot be delegated. He will need to take account of statutory requirements and will normally report on any significant weaknesses discovered during the audit.

Since internal audit is part of an organisation's control structure its effectiveness will need to be reviewed by external audit. This review needs to be seen by both parties as a necessary part of the working relationship.

External audit will need to be satisfied that the quality and planning of the internal audit coverage is satisfactory. Conversely internal audit should be satisfied as to the ability and efficiency of external audit since the success of co-operation must depend on the experience and expertise of both parties.

Forms of Co-operation

Information should be exchanged by making available audit plans, statements of systems and procedures, flow charts and audit reports.

Regular meetings between external and internal audit at which audit priorities, coverage generally, financial irregularities, fraud and other matters are discussed, should be held.

The participation of both external and internal auditors in training assignments and the formulation of joint training programmes should help to improve working relationships.

CLIENT DEPARTMENTS

STATEMENT

The relationship between the internal auditor and the management and staff of the departments subject to audit must be based on mutual confidence and understanding.

EXPLANATION

The Need for Good Relationships

It is the nature of internal audit to make searching enquiries, to carry out thorough tests and checks and, on occasion, to submit critical or controversial reports. It is therefore vital that management and staff at all levels have complete confidence in the integrity and independence of internal audit and that this should be reflected and maintained in good working relationships between auditors and client departments.

Obligations on the Internal Auditor

The auditor must be aware of the need for good relationships with staff at all levels in the department he is auditing. He should understand that there may be different reactions to his work at varying levels and that management styles may have an effect on the way he should approach his task. The desired relationship is most likely to be achieved through full understanding of the role of audit generally and of the particular audit task being undertaken. It is the auditor's duty to seek such understanding by open and friendly discussion and by calm and courteous persuasion. It should not normally be necessary to rely on the formal terms of reference and status of the audit department nor is an aggressive stance appropriate.

Planning the audit: The Statement on Planning and Control emphasises the need for the chief internal auditor to work in consultation with senior management in setting the audit plan. In arranging any audit, the auditor should bear in mind the need to advise and consult with management, both at headquarters and locally. This may well lead to the identification of areas of activity or topics on which audit coverage would be of particular value to management. Subject to any special factors requiring the audit visit to take place as planned, the internal audit department should be prepared to be responsive to management's requests or suggestions for alternative arrangements. Except on those occasions where an unannounced visit is part of the audit approach, audits should always be carried out by arrangement.

Conduct during an audit: The nature of an auditor's work means that he must be particularly careful to observe proper rules of behaviour. The auditor should remember that he is a visitor at each of the locations at which he conducts an audit and should be particularly aware of local protocol and such matters as punctuality, application to duty and general bearing.

The Privileged Nature of Audit

Audit is a privileged relationship between management and the auditor. Matters which arise during the course of an audit should not be discussed with third parties and attributable references must be avoided. If it is necessary at one location to refer to an occurrence at another, eg for purposes of illustration, this must be done on an anonymous basis.

Discussion of the Audit Report

The Statement on Reporting refers to the need for discussion with management when drafting and finalising the audit report. This requirement is not only to ensure that the report is factually based and takes account of comments expressed by management but is also an essential feature of the good relationship between client department and auditor. It is axiomatic that no report should be submitted formally without the knowledge of the department concerned.

OTHER REVIEW AGENCIES

STATEMENT

The internal auditor's relationship with other review agencies must be based on mutual confidence and understanding but must not compromise the relationship between the auditor and client department.

EXPLANATION

The Need for Co-operation

Work is undertaken by review agencies such as management services to improve and develop sound management and operations and is therefore to some extent complementary to that of the auditor. In planning and conducting audits the auditor will need to take account of the review agencies' work.

Certain information obtained during audits can be of considerable benefit to other review agencies and it will be in all parties' interest to make available information in order to avoid duplication of effort.

Scope and Operation of the Relationship

Whilst it is to the benefit of both the auditor and the review agencies to exchange information, this must not be to the detriment of auditor/client department relationships.

Review agencies' reports should be made available to the auditor both for information and for review and comment particularly where proposed systems changes may affect existing internal control arrangements.

Where audit reports draw attention to systems weaknesses it may be appropriate for review agencies to review and recommend detailed improvements. However before any audit report is released to a review agency the client department's formal approval should be obtained.

Regular meetings between the auditor and review agencies should take place to discuss present and future assignments and also any points arising from review agencies' and audit reports.

Glossary of Terms

The terms below have the meanings indicated when used in these Statements:

AUDIT	—The independent examination carried out by the internal audit department. Any matter which is under consideration by the internal auditor for which he may be required to express an opinion and report thereon.
AUDIT DEPARTMENT	—The internal audit section, internal audit, those engaged upon internal audit activities.
AUDITOR	—An individual member of the internal audit department carrying out an internal audit.
AUDIT PLAN	—The process whereby, on a long term, medium term and short term basis, the objectives defined for internal audit and the resources allocated to it are controlled.
AUDIT PROGRAMME	—The lists of tests and checks to be carried out during the course of an internal audit. In conjunction with flow charts, internal control questionnaires and other working papers it will form the record of work carried out and will be the basis of the internal audit report submitted to management.
CHIEF EXECUTIVE	—The chief official of the organisation: in central government, the accounting officer.
CHIEF INTERNAL AUDITOR	—The person who is responsible for the day-to-day management and activities of the internal audit department.
DIRECTOR OF FINANCE	—The head of the finance department, treasurer, financial administrator, chief finance officer, principal finance officer.
HEAD OF DEPARTMENT	—The person who has responsibility for departmental activities which may be the subject of audit, may include the director of finance.
MANAGEMENT	—A comprehensive term including all persons who have responsibility at various levels for activities which may be the subject of audit and to whom audit reports may be addressed.
MANAGEMENT BOARD	—The highest level of authority—board, council, policy resource committee.
SENIOR AUDIT STAFF	—Those responsible directly to the chief internal auditor or have responsibility for major aspects of audit work, includes team leaders.
SUPERVISOR	—The person responsible for supervising audit work, may be the chief internal auditor, senior audit staff, or other audit staff.

APPENDIX 2

Examples of basic audit programmes

Basic audit programme

WAGES/SALARIES

1. *Objectives*

1.1 To appraise the approved procedures and see that they are followed, that the payments made are correct and are in accordance with national/local agreements, that the records maintained are accurate and adequate, and proper security is exercised over collection, make-up, custody and pay-out of cash or cheques.

2. *Area of audit*

2.1 Commences where a wage/salary becomes due.
2.2 Finishes with the payment to the employee and posting in the financial records.

3. *Basic programme*

CONTROL

Review the system of control in order to verify the following:

3.1 That adequate and up-to-date records, covering all staff gradings and other entitlements, are maintained.
3.2 That there is an adequate system for the control of starters and leavers.
3.3 That adequate procedures exist for the authorisation of amendments to the record for new starters, leavers, salary changes, etc., and that these are properly actioned.
3.4 That daily, weekly and monthly time records (where appropriate) are properly certified.
3.5 That any additional payments (overtime, bonus, sick pay, etc.) are correctly calculated and supported by the correct documentation and are correctly authorised.
3.6 That control is exercised over input documentation in order to prevent duplication, loss or incorrect submission.
3.7 That there is control over all types of deduction and that these are paid, in due course, to the correct authority.
3.8 That gross and net pay totals are controlled in the financial records and

that pay-out procedures are clearly defined regarding security, identification and receipting.

Verify, by sample, or physically where necessary, the following:

3.9 The employment authorities and rates of pay (including additional payments, such as allowances).

3.10 The calculation of hours as booked on time records (if appropriate).

3.11 The amendments to rates of pay.

3.12 The calculation of gross pay.

3.13 That the deductions/refunds (statutory and voluntary) are properly authorised and correctly made.

3.14 That statutory and voluntary deductions are paid to the appropriate payees at the prescribed intervals.

3.15 The calculation of net pay.

3.16 The summarising of gross pay, deductions and net pay and the posting of totals to the financial records.

3.17 That the total wage/salary cheque(s) are reconciled with the payroll.

3.18 That procedures are adequate for payment by the following means:

3.18.1 BACS (Bankers Automated Clearing Services).

3.18.2 Cheque.

3.18.3 Cash.

3.18.4 Other – (please specify).

3.19 That security and other procedures, including identification, are adequate in respect of the following:

3.19.1 The collection and custody of bulk cash.

3.19.2 The make-up of net wages/salaries.

3.19.3 The pay-out of net wages/salaries.

3.19.4 The control and accounting for unclaimed wages/salaries.

3.20 That each employee has a national insurance record.

4. *Main areas of internal control*

4.1 There should be clearly defined details of duties and responsibilities for all personnel involved in payroll procedures.

4.2 There should be a proper authorisation for the engagement and discharge of employees.

4.3 There should be an adequate record covering all staff gradings and other entitlements and amendments, only made on the authorisation of an approved officer.

4.4 There should be a properly authorised notification for any payments made in addition to basic salary.

4.5 Voluntary deductions should only be made with the proper authority.

4.6 Adequate control accounts should be maintained for all deductions, and clearance of these is the responsibility of a senior officer.

4.7 There should be approval of the payroll by a responsible officer.

4.8 Wherever possible, salary payments should be by direct transfer.

4.9 The cheque(s) drawn to meet salary payments must equal the net payroll total.

4.10 Unclaimed wages/salary should be adequately controlled.

Basic audit programme

PAYROLL

Total number of staff on payroll	......	Payroll group or department	
Authorised establishment	......	Code reference	
Provision in estimates – current year	......	Week/month ended	
Actual expenditure to date	......	Total basic pay	
12 months equivalent	......	Total overtime	

No.	Individual probe	(1) Name: Ref:	(2) Name: Ref:	(3) Name: Ref:	(4) Name: Ref:	(5) Name: Ref:	(6) Name: Ref:	(7) Name: Ref:	(8) Name: Ref:	(9) Name: Ref:	(10) Name: Ref:
	Appointment and history records										
1.	Verify that post is within approved establishment										
2.	Ensure that post and grading for rate of pay were properly authorised.										
3.	Verify that recognised appointment procedure was followed.										
4.	If employee holds a second appointment, apply probes 1, 2 & 3 and include in following probes.										
5.	Ensure that current data held on magnetic tape, as evidenced by print-out, has been checked and agreed with current entries on the payroll record card.										
6.	Ensure that a permanent record is kept of the employee's service sufficient to cover the data required for possible future entry to superannuation scheme and possible payment due under redundancy payments scheme.										

		(1)	(2)	(3)	(4)	(5)	(6)	(7)	(8)	(9)	(10)
	Calculation of gross pay										
7.	Verify correctness of grade.										
8.	Verify that current rate of pay is correct and the basic weekly/monthly amount is correctly calculated.										
9.	Verify that all additional payments have been properly authorised and correctly calculated.										
10.	Ensure that a satisfactory record of overtime worked is maintained within the department.										
11.	If payment under review includes overtime, state total amount paid during last three months.										
12.	Ensure that satisfactory time records or attendance records are maintained.										
	Deductions and net pay										
13.	Verify that *all* deductions due to be made have actually been made and ensure they are correctly assessed and calculated. (*a*) Superannuation (*b*) National Insurance (*c*) PAYE (*d*) Union fees (*e*) Housing advance (*f*) Car loan										
	Subsidiary Records										
14.	Ensure that all advances, grants, loans, etc., which are recoverable or may be recoverable on leaving have been properly recorded on the payroll record card and magnetic tape store (see print-out).										

		(1)	(2)	(3)	(4)	(5)	(6)	(7)	(8)	(9)	(10)
15.	Ensure that the superannuation data given on payroll record card agrees with the superannuation personnel record and this agrees with the personal file.										
16.	Verify that the total of superannuation contributions for the last financial year as shown by the last payroll for that period agrees with the total amount shown on the computer print-out of contributions.										
17.	Verify that the total tax deductions and National Insurance contributions for the last ended year as shown on the final payroll agree with the figures shown on P35 computer substitute return.										
	Sickness										
18.	Ensure that a proper record is kept of all absences through sickness.										
19.	Verify that any sickness payments made during the past six months have been correctly calculated and the payments correctly recorded.										
	Payment of wages/salary										
20.	If paid in cash: (*a*) Ensure that the payroll has been signed with the employee's normal signature and that the paying officer has properly certified the payroll.										

		(1)	(2)	(3)	(4)	(5)	(6)	(7)	(8)	(9)	(10)
	(*b*) Ensure that a satisfactory record is kept of unclaimed wages and the disposal thereof.										
	(*c*) Ensure that the security for retention of unclaimed wages is good and that if they are not claimed within three weeks that they are repaid to bank.										
	(*d*) Ensure that the security arrangements for the custody of cash drawn from the bank and the make-up of pay are satisfactory.										
21.	If paid by cheque, verify that the paid cheque has been examined and found to be in order.										
22.	If pay is forwarded to a home address, ensure that there is a satisfactory reason for this and that the name and address appear in the Register of Electors.										
23.	If paid by cheque, ensure that if there were any special instructions with regard to despatch there were satisfactory reasons for such instructions.										
24.	If paid by bank credit, verify that the amount has been agreed with the print-out of the magnetic tape and that the total of the print-out agrees with the debit in the bank statement.										
	Leave										
25.	Ensure that a proper record of all absences on annual										

		(1)	(2)	(3)	(4)	(5)	(6)	(7)	(8)	(9)	(10)
	leave or special leave is maintained.										
26.	Ensure that the amount of leave taken as recorded during the last year was within the official entitlement or authorised if special leave.										
	Training										
27.	Ensure that all absences on post-entry training courses during the last twelve months have been properly recorded on the official training record for purposes of claiming grant (if applicable).										
28.	Ensure that all payments of fees, expenses or grants on training courses during the last twelve months have been properly recorded on the official training record.										

		ANSWER
29.	*Internal control* Ensure that the proper procedures were followed and the agreed internal check arrangements were fully documented and observed, i.e.,	
(*a*)	*Engaging employees* (*i*) Who engages employees? (*ii*) Are any employees engaged at the establishment where they will normally work? (*iii*) Are any persons engaged by the person who will be responsible for supervising them during their normal working day?	

		ANSWER
	(*iv*) Are there any special provisions operative for the engagement of temporary staff?	
(*b*)	*Time records (where appropriate)* (*i*) What time-recording system is in operation? (*ii*) Who completes the time sheet? (*iii*) Who certifies the time sheet and what are his daily relations with the employee? Is this the same person who engages staff? (*iv*) What independent check is made of the time sheet against the original time record?	
(*c*)	*Establishment control* (*i*) What control exists to ensure that the approved establishment is adhered to? (*ii*) Are there written authorities for the following: new employees; retirements, transfers, resignations, dismissals and changes; gradings; individual payroll deductions other than compulsory deductions? Are these documents certified by persons so authorised? Are specimen signatures of the authorisation held by salaries/wages section?	
(*d*)	Are appointment forms used? If so, how are they controlled? What control exists to show the salaries/wages section that an employee has been properly appointed?	
(*e*)	*Payment* (*i*) Who hands out wage/salary packets/cheques/slips? (*ii*) Is this the same person who also engages employees and/or certifies time sheets?	

(*f*)	*Other comments*	

Payroll probe carried out by:

Audit assistant.. Date...........

Audit team leader .... Date...........

Chief internal auditor.. Date...........

Man-day allocation

Allocated	Taken	Reasons for variation

Basic audit programme

CREDITORS – INVOICE PAYMENTS

1. *Objectives*

To ensure that the system and controls provide the following:

1.1 That all payments made are in respect of goods received and services rendered to the organisation and that these have been properly ordered.

2. *Area of audit*

2.1 Commences at the creditor's invoice.
2.2 Finishes at the cheque payments and postings to expenditure records.

3. *Basic programme*

Review the system of control, in order to ensure the following:

3.1 That all goods and services received are adequately covered by official documentation.
3.2 That all invoices paid are authorised in accordance with policy and that adequate procedures exist for the control of payments where no official order is issued.
3.3 That adequate control exists for the raising of, amendments to, and the deletion of standing periodic payments.
3.4 That control exists over the allocation and usage of creditors' reference numbers.
3.5 That control exists for the reconciliation of expenditure totals – invoice batch totals and cheque list totals.
3.6 That adequate division of duties exists in order to obviate the inclusion of 'dummy invoices'.

INVOICE PAYMENT RECORDS

By sample, verify the following:

3.7 That invoice certification is in accordance with laid down procedures.
3.8 That invoices paid are supported by copy orders, goods received or return notes, or other approved form of official documentation.
3.9 That approved authorisation exists for raising and amending periodic payments.
3.10 That there is no undue delay in the payment of invoices and recovery of credits.
3.11 That cash settlement discounts are being taken where applicable.
3.12 That the cost coding of invoices is correct and agrees with expenditure records.
3.13 That cheque payment records agree with invoice batch control register totals and expenditure totals.

GENERAL

3.14 Examine records and procedures and verify that controls exist which cover payments made against documents raised internally.
3.15 Examine procedures for control over the usages and stocks of unused cheques.
3.16 Verify that adequate controls exist which cover special or quick payments made manually.
3.17 Examine the control over payments which are made against duplicate invoices and reasons for so doing.

4. *Main areas of internal control*

4.1 There should be an adequate system of internal check with proper controls and division of duties.
4.2 Lists of approved signatories should be available covering all employees who have the authority to authorise payments.
4.3 Proper procedures should exist for control over the raising of, and amendments to, periodic payments.
4.4 There should be adequate and independent control over the usage and stocks of cheques, particularly where pre-signed cheques are used.
4.5 There should be a control register of creditors. Reference numbers and the issue and deletion of numbers should be strictly controlled.
4.6 There should be a periodic review of all unprocessed invoices.
4.7 A procedure for the cancellation of paid invoices should be in operation.
4.8 Adequate procedural checks should be carried out in all cases where payment is requested against duplicate/copy invoices.
4.9 There should be control procedures for the raising of cheques against pro-forma invoices/cheque requisitions which are raised internally.

Basic audit programme

CREDITORS

Payee	Batch No. .....
Brief details of payment	Date of payment ...... Amount £
	Date of invoice ....

Provision in estimates	Formal agreement if any
Actual to date	Committee minute

(1) Individual probes (if a probe is not applicable then mark N/A in tick column)	(2) If answer as shown below tick here	(3) If answer is not as in column (2) enter below with comments
Ordering		
1. Was an official order used?	Yes	
(*a*) If so, was it made out before purchase?	Yes	
(*b*) Do quantities and qualities agree with invoice?	Yes	
(*c*) Has the copy order been marked as 'passed for payment' with the date?	Yes	
(*d*) Is the person signing the order authorised to do so?	Yes	
2. Is authority to order restricted to specified officers?	Yes	
(Please supply brief details.)	→	
Are orders actually signed by these officers?	Yes	
3. Are order books adequately controlled?	Yes	
4. Are orders supported by requisition?	Yes	
5. What is the procedure for dealing with verbal orders/emergency orders/open orders, etc.? (Please give brief details.)	→	

(1) Individual probes (if a probe is not applicable then mark N/A in tick column)	(2) If answer as shown below tick here		(3) If answer is not as in column (2) enter below with comments
Receiving			
6. (*a*) Did the person who signed 'goods received' in the certification actually receive and check the goods?	Yes		
(*b*) (*i*) If not, did he before initialling check with a delivery note or goods received note signed by the person receiving?	Yes		
(*ii*) If answer to last probe is 'yes', have you seen the delivery note and verified the identity of the person signing?	Yes		
7. If it is an item where delivery note would normally be sent, check the delivery note with the invoice.	Checked		
8. If it is a stock item then (*a*) check the entry in the records, and	Checked		
(*b*) verify present physical stock.	Checked		
9. If it is an inventory item then either (*a*) check entry in inventory and verify existence, or	Checked		
(*b*) note in appropriate file for physical checking on next visit.	Noted		
10. If the item should be entered in a goods received book, then check the entry.	Checked		
11. Is the person signing the 'goods received' certification or delivery note the same person who signed the official order (or who gave the order, if no official order)?	No		

(1) Individual probes (if a probe is not applicable then mark N/A in tick column)	(2) If answer as shown below tick here		(3) If answer is not as in column (2) enter below with comments
Certification and prices			
12. (*a*) Is the invoice arithmetically correct?	Yes		
(*b*) Were tenders or quotations obtained?	Yes		
If so, are prices in accordance therewith?	Yes		
(*c*) If quotations were obtained:			
(*i*) Was the lowest accepted	Yes		
(*ii*) If not, was an appropriate report made to the Committee?	Yes		
(*d*) If the cost of work was estimated, does the actual show an increase?	No		
(*e*) If the item purchased is an annual contract of any other department:			
(*i*) Is the price paid higher than the rate applicable to the other department?	No		
(*ii*) If the price is lower, has the other department been notified?			
(*iii*) At what prices do neighbouring organisations obtain similar goods?			
(*f*) (*i*) Is the coding allocation correct?	Yes		
(*ii*) Is the budget head overspent?	No		
(*iii*) If capital, has an entry been made in capital ledger?	Yes		
(*g*) Have all possible discounts and allowances been deducted?	Yes		
13. (*a*) Is there an approved list of certifying officers?	Yes		

(1) Individual probes (if a probe is not applicable then mark N/A in tick column)	(2) If answer as shown below tick here		(3) If answer is not as in column (2) enter below with comments
(*b*) Are invoices actually certified by these officers?	Yes		
(*c*) Is the certification by facsimile signature?	Yes		
If so, are the stamps in safe custody?	Yes		
14. Does the certifying officer			
(*a*) Order supplies?	No		
(*b*) Receive supplies?	No		
15. (*a*) Have all the appropriate certifications in the 'block' been completed?	Yes		
(*b*) Have the initials, etc., of persons certifying in the 'block' been identified?	Yes		
(*c*) Have the persons so identified the necessary authority to certify?	Yes		
(*d*) Has VAT been dealt with correctly?	Yes		
General			
16. (*a*) Is the invoice addressed to the organisation?	Yes		
(*b*) Is the invoice on the creditor's own bill-head?	Yes		
If not,			
(*i*) Are there any suspicious features revealed by examination of paid cheque?	No		
(*ii*) Does the name and address appear in the telephone directory *or*	Yes		
Register of Electors?	Yes		
(*iii*) Does question 11 apply	No		
17. Is there a possibility of income being due to the organisation?	No		

(1) Individual probes (if a probe is not applicable then mark N/A in tick column)	(2) If answer as shown below tick here		(3) If answer is not as in column (2) enter below with comments
18. Is the quantity ordered			
(*a*) excessive having regard to requirements or existing stocks?	No		
(*b*) insufficient having regard to possible 'bulk purchase' savings?	No		
19. Is there sufficient description on the invoice to identify clearly the items purchased?	Yes		
20. Has this description been inserted by the supplier? (If not, by whom?)	Yes		
21. (*a*) Do the name and amount on the paid chequc agree with the details			
(*i*) on the invoice, and	Yes		
(*ii*) in the copy cash book?	Yes		
(*b*) Are there any suspicious or undesirable features with regard to the person to whom the cheque is made payable? (see question 16 (*b*).)	No		
22. Has there been any prolonged and undue delay in either the rendering of the invoice or passing the account for payment?	No		
If so, state reasons.	→	→	
23. If the payment was made as an 'urgent payment' was this justified?	Yes		
24. If the item is a periodical payment, check the 'p.p.' entry for accuracy and watch duplicate payment possibility.	Checked		
25. Were there any specific instructions for handing the cheque to any person?	No		
If so, to whom and why?	→	→	

(1) Individual probes (if a probe is not applicable then mark N/A in tick column)	(2) If answer as shown below tick here		(3) If answer is not as in column (2) enter below with comments
Procedures generally			
26. Have standing orders and financial regulations been complied with?	Yes		
27. Any comments on internal control or procedures generally whether directly or indirectly concerned with the payment.	→		
Observations			
28. In answering the questions enumerated in this questionnaire it may be necessary to ask supplementary questions to establish the full facts. Similarly, there may be significant information arising from this inquiry not specifically covered here, but nevertheless relevant. The facts should be recorded.			

Audit probe carried out by:

Audit assistant .... Date...........

Audit team leader.. Date...........

Chief internal auditor .... Date...........

Basic audit programme

CASH COLLECTION

1. *Objectives*

1.1 To verify that the procedures for the security, collection, receipting and recording of all cash are adequate and in accordance with procedures.
1.2 To ensure that all cash collected is correctly banked without delay.
1.3 To ensure that the system is adequate, in order that the postings to the relevant accounts will be carried out correctly and promptly.

2. *Area of audit*

2.1 Commences at the receipt of cash at all types of collection points.
2.2 Finishes at the banking of the cash and posting to the accounting records, and the carrying out of a regular reconciliation of all bank accounts.

3. *Basic programme*

CONTROL

3.1 Review and test that the system provides for control of all types of receipts.
3.2 Verify that the system ensures the adequate recording of all monies received from all sources, including postal remittances.
3.3 Verify that the system means that collections are banked without delay on a daily basis.
3.4 Review the system of internal control and check that there is an adequate division of duties within the cash section.

RECEIPT CONTROL, CASH COLLECTION AND BANKING RECORDS

By sample, verify the following:

3.5 The control over stocks and issues and the daily usage of manual type receipts.
3.6 The control exercised over the usage of receipt books and machines.
3.7 That cash receipted from all types of sources has been correctly recorded.
3.8 That collections, including cheques, have been banked without delay.
3.9 That cashiers' and collectors' overs and shorts are reported to management for action where necessary.
3.10 The transfers from National Giro and ensure that the control exercised over both cleared and uncleared remittances is adequate.
3.11 That transfers received from bank Giros are adequately recorded and controlled.
3.12 The summary of collections and ensure that control is adequate.
3.13 That the system for credit posting is adequately controlled and that any unposted/unidentified cash is recorded and controlled.

GENERAL

3.14 Examine and ensure that the system of cash collection by agencies is adequate and that bankings are made without delay.

3.15 Ascertain that National Giro and night safe facilities are used in order to reduce the cash held overnight.

3.16 Examine arrangements for the banking of cash collections under contract security services.

3.17 Verify, in cases where payments can be made from collections, that these are adequately covered by documentation.

3.18 Verify, where cash is paid over from one cashier/collector to a supervisor, etc., that there is a clear indication of the discharge of responsibility.

4. *Main areas of internal control*

4.1 It should be the responsibility of an independent person to control the stocks and daily usage of manual type receipts.

4.2 There should be control over receipts issued by both receipt books and receipting machines.

4.3 There should be a reconciliation of daily collections and bankings.

4.4 The system should provide for any cash in hand and unbanked from the previous day to be isolated and to be seen to be banked.

4.5 Cheque payments should be identified to obviate 'teeming and lading'.

4.6 The system should provide for the 'crossing' of cheques, postal orders, etc., when received.

Basic audit programme

TRAVELLING AND SUBSISTENCE ALLOWANCES

1. *Objectives*

To ensure that allowances for the use of employees' private cars on the organisation's business, and subsistence claims, are properly authorised, and that payments are made in accordance with the organisation's scheme.

2. *Area of audit*

2.1 Commences with approval as an authorised or casual user.
2.2 Finishes with payment to the employee.

3. *Basic programme*

CONTROL

3.1 To review and test the procedures for the authorisation of payment of travelling and subsistence allowances and the verification of current insurance.
3.2 To review and test the procedures for the submission of claims for mileage incurred and subsistence claimed.

CLAIMS

By sample, verify the following:

3.3 That the vehicle for which the car allowance is claimed is registered in the name of the officer concerned. (This check will have to be done via the Driving Vehicle Licensing Centre at Swansea to obtain the name and address of the owner from the registration documents.)
3.4 That the essential user or casual user is properly authorised.
3.5 That the vehicle cubic capacity agrees with the registration details.
3.6 The reasonableness of the claim and also check that it is properly completed in accordance with instructions.
3.7 That a claim is properly authorised by an approved officer.
3.8 That the rate per mile, lump sum (where applicable) and subsistence allowance are correct.
3.9 That the calculations are correct.
3.10 Where speedo. readings are available from a supplementary source of information, confirm that some private mileage is incurred each day and at weekends. In other words, there should be gaps between the speedo. readings shown one day for official use and another.
3.11 The payment to employees.

GENERAL

3.12 Examine for nil mileages and enquire into reasons.
3.13 Review the need for essential user status where little mileage is incurred.

4. *Main areas of internal control*

4.1 Procedures are provided for proper authorisation of essential and casual users.

4.2 Claims are submitted that show details of the mileage incurred, the subsistence claimed and the reasons which enable authorising officers to approve.

4.3 The approval of claims is given by designated officers.

4.4 Management information is provided to enable the scheme to be kept under review and also to bring cases, where low mileages or large mileages are claimed, to the attention of chief officers, for re-appraisal of authorisation.

Basic audit programme

TRANSPORT

1. *Objectives*

To verify the following:

1.1 That proper management controls operate regarding the purchasing, leasing, hire and disposal of vehicles and plant.
1.2 That the cost of repair and maintenance programmes is being effectively monitored.
1.3 That control is being exercised over vehicle and plant running costs, including fuel, tyres, batteries and spare parts.
1.4 That control is being exercised over the utilisation of vehicles and plant.
1.5 That the computerised vehicle job costing system recharge to service departments is working satisfactorily.

2. *Area of audit*

2.1 Commences with vehicle acquisition.
2.2 Finishes with vehicle disposal.

3. *Basic programme*

ACQUISITION AND DISPOSAL OF VEHICLES AND PLANT

3.1 Review procedures for authorisation of addition/replacement vehicles.
3.2 Review procedures for disposal of vehicles no longer required.

By sample, verify the following:

3.3 That all purchases of new vehicles are authorised in accordance with procedures.
3.4 That reasons for additional/replacement vehicles are valid in accordance with policy.
3.5 Tenders received for purchase of vehicles.
3.6 That disposal of vehicles are displaced in accordance with procedures.
3.7 That credit is received for disposed vehicles.
3.8 The plant register entries and depreciation rates or entries in the leasing register.

HIRED VEHICLES

For a sample period, verify the following:

3.9 That hire is authorised in accordance with policy.
3.10 That quotations for hire are obtained.
3.11 That rates and details of hire invoices are correct.
3.12 That economic use is being made of hired vehicles i.e., that vehicles are not idle whilst hired transport in use.

MAINTENANCE OF VEHICLES

3.13 Review the policy for servicing and repairs.

Inspect a sample of vehicle history records to verify the following:

3.14 That servicing is carried out regularly in accordance with the programme.
3.15 That planned inspection of vehicles is carried out in accordance with the programme.
3.16 That where repairs or maintenance are carried out by outside firms, this is in accordance with policy.
3.17 That the MOT test requirements are met.
3.18 The extent of supervisory checks on work done (both by own labour and outside firms).
3.19 That insurance claims are made in case of accident damage.
3.20 That the system for recording expenditure and maintenance is operating satisfactorily.
3.21 Compare charges/costs for jobs with the standard charges of private garages.

VEHICLE RUNNING

By sample, verify the following:

3.22 The use of agency cards and petrol purchases from outside garages. Also verify that the receipts and issues of petrol, derv and oil from stocks are properly controlled and recorded.
3.23 That tyre requirements are in accordance with arrangements.
3.24 That the issue of vehicle spares, etc., from stocks and direct purchases are properly controlled and recorded, paying particular attention to attractive items.
3.25 That tax and insurance charges and appropriate refunds are obtained.
3.26 That drivers' record books are properly completed.

USE OF VEHICLES

3.27 Appraise supervisory arrangements.
3.28 Examine arrangements for routing vehicles, delivery areas, etc.
3.29 Appraise suitability of vehicle used.
3.30 Appraise and test procedures for authorising vehicles to be taken home.
3.31 Examine use of cars and verify recharge to users where appropriate.
3.32 Review and assess time spent 'off the road' and the reasons therefore.
3.33 Examine vehicle use statistics and test the accuracy of management information.

GARAGING

3.34 Appraise adequacy of premises.
3.35 Appraise security arrangements.
3.36 Examine custody of spares and tools.

4. *Main areas of internal control*

4.1 In addition to normal expenditure authorisation procedures, there should be a system of request and justification for additional or hired vehicles reviewed by the transport manager.

4.2 The system should provide for review and justification of the continued hiring of vehicles.

4.3 There should be a recognised policy for disposal of vehicles and a control that the appropriate credits are received.

4.4 Proper procedures should exist for the regular obtaining of quotations for hire.

4.5 Adequate records should be kept to ensure vehicles are called forward for servicing and for their inspection to comply with legislative requirements.

4.6 Proper control should be exercised over the purchase and issue of fuel stocks and of the use of agency cards. Independent dippings of fuel stocks held should be carried out regularly and any discrepancies certified by a designated officer.

4.7 Proper control should be exercised over spares, tyres and other stocks.

4.8 Suitable management information should be prepared to enable a constant review of utilisation and costs of the fleet to be carried out.

Basic audit programme

SCHOOL

This form is for use as a guide to the areas which should be examined and its contents and scope must be treated as confidential.

The form cannot be designed to be exhaustive; therefore it must not be followed to the exclusion of initiative, current conditions or audit principles.

School	*Code*			
Date of audit	C	=	Completed	
Head	R	=	See Report	
Secretary	NA	=	Not applicable	
Audit assistant(s)	NE	=	Not examined	
	T	=	Test checked	

1. *Objectives*

To review, appraise and report on:

1.1 The soundness, adequacy and application of financial and other management controls.

1.2 The extent to which the authority's assets and interests are accounted for and safeguarded from losses of all kinds arising from:
(*a*) fraud and other offences;
(*b*) waste, extravagance and inefficient administration, poor value for money or other cause.

1.3 The extent of compliance with, relevance to and financial effect of established policies, plans and procedures.

1.4 The suitability and reliability of financial and other management data developed within the organisation.

	Code	*Initials*
2. *Pre-audit*		
2.1 Arrange visit with Head/Secretary.		
2.2 Obtain:		
(*i*) School audit file, noting any items requiring follow-up action.		
(*ii*) Latest available return of meals supplied.		
(*iii*) Cash advances		
(*a*) School £		
(*b*) Kitchen £		
(*c*) Special activities £		
(*d*) Domestic science agreed loss £		

Code	Initials

2.3 Compare meals supplied with those paid for (at least three months).

Month	Return of meals supplied	Return of meals paid for

2.4 Obtain:
(*i*) Audit record card.
(*ii*) School fund record card.

2.5 Extract latest school meals costs:

Period		
	School	County average
Food		
Wages Cook-in-charge Kitchen staff		

2.6 Obtain domestic science account returns.

2.7 Obtain latest income and expenditure figures per establishment tabulation.

2.8 Extract voucher/creditor numbers for some purchases of equipment and furniture; obtain copies of the paid accounts and list full details.

2.9 Extract expenditure on:
Woodwork – total expend. 19 £
Metalwork – total expend. 19 £

2.10 Extract pupil/teacher ratio and average for that type of school

School –

Average –

	Code	Initials
2.11 Extract information on fuel consumption for last three years and current year.		

Type of fuel	19	19	19	19
Electricity (units)				
Gas (therms)				
Oil (galls)				
Solid fuel Coal/coke (tons)				

2.12 Obtain names, hours worked, posts of all teachers including authorised establishment.
2.13 Obtain names and hours worked of clerical assistants, caretakers, school meals staff, cleaners, etc., and a copy of previous weeks' weekly time sheets.
2.14 Note any rent or other deductions.
2.15 Extract needlework debit.
2.16 Obtain latest Department of Education & Science (DES) form 7 when required.

3. *Basic programme*

3.1 *Previous reports*
3.1.1 Examine previous audit reports and replies, noting any items requiring follow-up action. (Note: this should be undertaken before visit is made.)

3.2 *Cash and security*
3.2.1 Check all cash in hand and agree with records.
3.2.2 Enquire into arrangements for security of cash, especially overnight.
3.2.3 Examine regularity of bankings and ensure cash held is kept to a minimum.
3.2.4 Examine safeguards against teeming and lading between funds.
3.2.5 Enquire into procedure for transport of cash between home and bank.

3.3 *Imprest account*
3.3.1 Reconcile imprest account.
3.3.2 Ensure that imprest account is used only for approved purposes.

		Code	Initials
3.3.3	Ensure that advance is sufficient, but not more than required.		
3.3.4	Examine items of expenditure being financed through imprest account and report any irregular items.		
3.4	*School meals*		
3.4.1	Ensure that the system for collection of school meals income in use is adequate.		
3.4.2	Meal registers – ensure properly kept and balanced weekly, test check records and balancing and trace to bank and return of meals supplied.		
3.4.3	Daily cash collection – ensure arrangements for collecting cash are adequate, test-check cash received to meals served, examine trend of income.		
3.4.4	Tickets – ensure there are adequate arrangements for issuing tickets, collecting them at lunchtime and destroying them in due course. Examine records and test-check tickets issued with cash collect.		
3.4.5	Check the last six weeks' collections to bank.		
3.4.6	Agree the last return of meals supplied to meal registers.		
3.4.7	Compare return of meals supplied with cook's return of meals supplied and enquire into differences.		
3.4.8	Examine daily order system and ensure return of meals supplied and return of meals paid for figures are computed independently.		
3.4.9	Examine authority for free meals and test-check with attendance register.		
3.4.10	Examine records of staff meals and enquire into level of free meals.		
3.4.11	When possible, observe the system in operation at lunchtime for the physical count of pupils taking meals. Ensure there is proper control to prevent unauthorised entry to dining room.		

Code	Initials

3.5 *Sales*

3.5.1 Examine records, bankings and, where appropriate, percentage return for:
(*i*) Needlework
(*ii*) Woodwork
(*iii*) Metalwork
(*iv*) Pottery
(*v*) Lettings
(*vi*) Domestic science
(*vii*) Gardening/rural science
(*viii*) Scrap
(*ix*) Swill
(*x*) Private telephone calls
(*xi*) Other – specify

3.5.2 Examine requisitions for types of purchases which might result in income.

3.5.3 Enquire into cases where sales income might be expected but not received.

3.6 *Staff*

3.6.1 Examine procedure for appointment of staff, certification of time sheets and payment of wages/salary and report on weaknesses.

3.6.2 Verify audit record of staff by physical existence (where possible):
(*i*) All teaching staff – full-time and part-time
(*ii*) All cleaning and kitchen staff
(*iii*) Clerical assistants, caretaker(s), lab technicians, etc.
Where it is not possible to verify physical existence, reference should be made to school timetables, school return of staff, etc.

3.6.3 Ensure part-time teaching staff are only paid for the number of hours actually worked.

3.6.4 Examine procedure for unpaid wages/salary.

3.6.5 Check as far as possible that there appears to be no overstaffing. Ensure that approved establishment and allocation of hours is not exceeded.

3.6.6 Inspect current time sheets and time book, verify that they are being kept correctly and that there is a check on time-keeping, etc.

		Code	*Initials*
3.6.7	Verify deductions are being made for appropriate items (e.g. rent of caretaker for staff housing).		
3.6.8	Check allocation of clerical hours to school number and ensure hours worked are within approved scale.		
3.6.9	Compare cleaning hours at school to the floor area and check with approved scales.		
3.6.10	Check kitchen staff hours to the number of meals provided and the approved scale.		
3.6.11	Ensure head teacher's salary is calculated correctly – in accordance with school population.		
3.7	*Kitchen*		
3.7.1	Enquire into and investigate excessive unit costs.		
3.7.2	Physically check a sample of selected stock items.		
3.7.3	Inspect order/goods received books to see that purchases are reasonable.		
3.7.4	Ensure that purchases are being made from Council's approved suppliers at the contract price. Ensure food supplies are checked for quality and quantity. Enquire into any complaints about the quality of food and the action taken.		
3.7.5	Inspect menus and check whether these correspond with food ordered and whether meals provided seem reasonable.		
3.7.6	Inspect weekly issues book to see that issues are reasonable.		
3.7.7	Inspect physical stock to see that stocks and stores are not carried in excess of reasonable requirements.		
3.7.8	Check on security and control to see that stocks are locked up when stock room is not in use.		
3.7.9	Examine procedure for notification of meals supplied and verify that numbers catered for tally with the number entitled to a meal and ensure there is a system whereby the cook is notified of variations.		
3.7.10	Ascertain how many staff are catered for and whether they are entitled to meals.		

		Code	Initials
3.7.11	Ascertain whether meals are supplied to any visitors and whether payment is made.		
3.7.12	Check on arrangements for disposal of waste and any payment for pigswill.		
3.7.13	Ensure that staff are not allowed to bring shopping bags into the kitchen.		
3.7.14	Compare items on sample of paid invoices with stock book to ensure stock book is being used correctly.		
3.8	*Inventory*		
3.8.1	Inspect records of furniture and equipment, etc., and ensure it is up to date.		
3.8.2	Check on items recently purchased as per extracts and requisitions.		
3.8.3	Test-check physical stock.		
3.8.4	Ensure that surplus, obsolete and unserviceable equipment has been disposed of correctly. Pay particular attention to write-offs – examine authority.		
3.8.5	Check recent purchases to inventory to ensure record is kept up to date.		
3.8.6	Examine level of equipment, etc., maintained by school and report on excessive stocks, etc.		
3.9	*Fuel*		
3.9.1	Examine fuel consumption record for last three years and investigate reasons for any apparent increase.		
3.9.2	Check that purchases of fuel are obtained from the Council's approved suppliers.		
3.9.3	Ensure that caretaker or his nominee is present when fuel is delivered and meter readings, tanker dips, etc., are checked.		
3.9.4	Enquire into any complaints about the quality of the fuel and the action taken.		
3.9.5	Enquire into system for control of heating levels, periods in use, etc., and report any evidence of excess temperatures, excessive hours in use and general 'poor housekeeping'.		

	Code	Initials
3.10 *Accounts*		
3.10.1 School fund and any other school voluntary accounts – inspect certificate that accounts are being prepared and audited.		
3.10.2 School cruise – verify existence and check income receipt books to bank, etc.		
3.10.3 Special activities – verify existence and operation.		
3.10.4 Rural science – verify existence and operation.		
3.10.5 Ensure registration card up to date.		
3.11 *Orders*		
3.11.1 Examine local order books (if applicable) and ensure they are only used for minor purchases.		
3.11.2 Examine control over issue of orders, receipt of goods, marking off orders and submission of account for payment.		
3.11.3 Enquire into any items of an unusual or excessive nature.		
3.11.4 Scrutinise order book and watch for excessive consumption of items.		
3.12 *Building maintenance costs*		
3.12.1 Examine expenditure on building maintenance and investigate any items of an unusal or expensive nature.		
3.12.2 Ensure that school only issues orders for emergency work and then up to £50.		
3.12.3 Enquire into any contracts for decorating, minor building works and ensure Head can confirm that work was carried out accordingly to the specification.		
3.12.4 Ensure approved contractors have been used.		
3.13 *Transport*		
3.13.1 Observe various contract buses/taxis, etc., arriving at school and ensure that the number are in accordance with the contract.		
3.13.2 Ensure that all income has been received and banked for assisted transport passes sent to school by Area Office.		

	Code	Initials
3.14 *Miscellaneous*		
3.14.1 Compare pupil/teacher ratio with County average.		
3.14.2 Ensure that a record of private telephone calls is kept. Inspect receipts and trace to bank. Examine reasonableness of telephone expenditure.		
3.14.3 Ensure examination entry fee is paid and booked by pupils retaking examinations.		
3.14.4 Examine registers for out-County pupils and ensure that those at school on the appropriate day in January are included in the out-County claim.		
3.14.5 Test numbers of pupils recorded on DES form 7.		

Audit assistant .... Date....................

Audit team leader...................................... Date....................

Chief internal auditor .... Date....................

Basic cash audit programme

TECHNICAL COLLEGE

Auditors ....
.... College
.... Date of audit ....

Item	*Audit category*	*By (initials)*	*Extent of check (dates, nos., etc.)*
Pre-audit information			
A. Particulars of current imprest including latest available claim paid.	1		
B. Details of controlled stationery issued.	1		
C. Details of telephone accounts paid for call-boxes.	1		

Item	*Audit category*	*By (initials)*	*Extent of check (dates, nos., etc.)*
Audit			
1. *Imprest account*			
(a) Verify balance in hand.	1		
(b) Verify balance at bank.	1		
(c) Check sub-imprests and floats.	1		
(d) Check entries with voucher.	2		
(e) Follow up large or unusual items.	2		
2. *Controlled stationery* Account for a selected sample of controlled stationery.	1		
3. *Receipts to bank*			
(a) Test-check receipts to cash book.	1		
(b) Test-check bankings to bank pay-in book.	1		
(c) Ensure cash and cheques paid in promptly.	1		
4. *Fees income*			
(a) Obtain all registers and enrolment forms.	1		
(b) Test-check from register control to ensure that all registers have been received.	1		
(c) Test-check that receipt numbers are shown against each name.	1		
(d) Test-check numbers shown to enrolment forms.	1		
(e) From enrolment forms test-check fees charged to receipts and invoices.	1		
5. *Shop/sale of equipment*			
(a) Check all sales money has been accounted for.	1		
(b) Check that cash has been paid in promptly.	1		

Item	*Audit category*	*By (initials)*	*Extent of check (dates, nos., etc.)*
(c) Ensure reconciliations carried out periodically between purchases and sales.	2		
6. *Catering department sales* From stores records and staff records ensure any income due is being collected and paid in promptly.	1		
7. *Bar*			
(a) Ensure bar reconciliation carried out periodically.	1		
(b) Evaluate stock usage for a period and compare with income.	2		
(c) Test bar sales to cash income sheets and to cash book.	1		
8. *Hairdressing*			
(a) Ensure adequate system of accounting for cash collected is being operated.	2		
(b) Test prices charged with scale of charges.	1		
(c) Test cash income paid into cashier and banked.	1		
9. *Refectory*			
(a) Test check all income shown on till rolls and daily record of sales banked.	1		
(b) Ensure income is received for all selling points.	1		
(c) Where separate selling points made it possible, evaluate sales with income (e.g. vending machines etc.).	2		
(d) Cash up selected tills at convenient opportunity.	1		

Item	*Audit category*	*By (initials)*	*Extent of check (dates, nos., etc.)*
(*e*) Examine latest available refectory management information, compare with income/expenditure and previous period.	3		
(*f*) Where possible compare takings of cashiers.	2		
10. *Telephone call-boxes* Compare accumulated income per cash book with telephone charges.	2		
11. *Photocopying*			
(*a*) Calculate total number of copies issued and compare with total of 'sold' copies and 'official' copies.	3		
(*b*) Verify that income received for all sold copies.	3		
(*c*) Ensure official copies properly authorised.	3		
12. *Departmental and miscellaneous income*			
(*a*) Investigate for all other potential sources of income (e.g. sale of scrap, publications).	1		
(*b*) Verify reasonable amount of income received.	1		

Basic audit programme (other than cash)

TECHNICAL COLLEGE

Auditors ....
.... College
.... Date of audit ....

Item	*Audit category*	*By (initials)*	*Extent of check (dates, nos., etc.)*
Pre-audit information			
A. File-tab print-out of all employees at establishment.	1		
B. Particulars of current imprest.	1		
C. Details of controlled stationery issued.	1		
D. Paid accounts in audit file.	1		
E. Selection of part-time lecturers' claim forms.	1		
F. Obtain details of any unusual items or trends of income and expenditure.	1		
G. Details of telephone accounts paid for call-boxes.	1		

Item	*Audit category*	*By (initials)*	*Extent of check (dates, nos., etc.)*
Audit			
1. *Imprest account*			
(*a*) Verify balance in hand.	1		
(*b*) Verify balance at bank.	1		
(*c*) Check sub-imprests and floats.	1		
(*d*) Check entries with vouchers.	2		
(*e*) Follow up large or unusual items.	2		
2. *Controlled stationery* Account for all controlled stationery.	1		
3. *Receipts cash book*			
(*a*) Test-check receipts to receipts cash book.	1		
(*b*) Test-check bankings to bank pay-in book.	1		
(*c*) Carry out teeming/ lading check.	1		
4. *Fees income*			
(*a*) Obtain all registers.	1		
(*b*) Test-check from register control to ensure that all have been received.	1		
(*c*) Ensure receipt numbers are shown against each name.	1		
(*d*) Test-check numbers shown to copy receipts and invoices where appropriate.	1		
(*e*) Obtain enrolment forms and test-check fees charged for students shown on registers.	1		
(*f*) Test-check from enrolment forms to invoices.	1		
5. *Extra district claims*			
(*a*) Test-check enrolment forms for 'out-County' students.	1		

Item	Audit category	By (initials)	Extent of check (dates, nos., etc.)
(b) Check 'out-County' students to computer tab.	1		
(c) Test-check calculation of hours in registers to computer tab.	1		
6. *Shop/sale of equipment*			
(a) Check all sales money has been accounted for.	1		
(b) Check that cash has been paid in promptly.	1		
(c) Ensure reconciliations carried out periodically between purchases and sales.	1		
(d) Test-check goods purchased (from Treasurer's paid accounts) to shop records.	3		
7. *Catering department sales*			
(a) Obtain stores records for suitable period.	2		
(b) Obtain staff records for same period and ensure all requisitions received.	2		
(c) From staff records ensure any income due is being collected and paid in promptly.	2		
8. *Bar*			
(a) Ensure bar reconciliation carried out periodically.	1		
(b) Evaluate stock usage for a period and compare with income.	1		
(c) Test bar sales to cash income sheets and to cash book.	1		
(d) Test check purchases from Treasurer's paid accounts to bar records.	2		

Item	*Audit category*	*By (initials)*	*Extent of check (dates, nos., etc.)*
9. *Hairdressing*			
(a) Ensure reasonable system of accounting for cash collected is being operated.	2		
(b) Test prices charged with scale of charges.	2		
(c) Test cash income paid into cashier and banked.	1		
10. *Refectory*			
(a) Test-check all income shown on till rolls and daily record of sales banked.	1		
(b) Ensure income is received from all selling points.	1		
(c) Where separate selling points make it possible, evaluate sales with income (e.g. vending machines, etc.).	2		
(d) Cash up selected tills at convenient opportunity.	2		
(e) Examine latest available refectory management information, compare with income/expenditure and previous period.	2		
(f) Trace selection of paid Treasurer's invoices into stock records.	2		
(g) Where possible compare takings of cashiers.	2		
(h) Ensure current supplies are being obtained on best possible terms.	3		
11. *Ordering procedure*			
(a) Examine orders for reasonableness of purchase.	1		
(b) Ensure procedure is being correctly adhered to.	1		

Item	Audit category	By (initials)	Extent of check (dates, nos., etc.)
12. *Examination fees*			
(a) Select request for payment for exam fees.	3		
(b) Check amount with college copy of exam entry form.	3		
(c) Check, if appropriate, student has paid exam fees.			
(d) Check that external exam students have paid local fee.	3		
13. *Telephone call-boxes* Accumulated income per cash book compared with British Telecom charges.	2		
14. *Photocopying*			
(a) Calculate total number of copies issued and compare with total of 'sold' copies and 'official' copies.	3		
(b) Verify that income received for all sold copies.	3		
(c) Ensure official copies properly authorised.	3		
15. *Lettings*			
(a) From college diary or similar record, obtain details of lettings of parts of colleges.	2		
(b) Test-check that invoices have been raised.	2		
(c) Ensure charges levied are in agreement with current scale of charges, or variations approved by governors.	2		

Item	*Audit category*	*By (initials)*	*Extent of check (dates, nos., etc.)*
16. *Departmental and miscellaneous income*			
(*a*) Investigate for all other potential sources of income (e.g. sale of scrap, publications).	2		
(*b*) Verify reasonable amount of income received.	2		
17. *Inventory*			
(*a*) Verify inventory kept up to date and that regular inventory checks take place.	1		
(*b*) Check to the inventory items selected from paid accounts.	1		
(*c*) Physically test-check items purchased.	2		
(*d*) Physically test-check other items shown in inventory.	2		
(*e*) Ensure correct procedure followed up for items written off or sold.	2		
(*f*) Trace any income from sales	3		
18. *Salaries and wages*			
(*a*) Test-check existence of staff shown on file-tab print-out.	2		
(*b*) From timetables/registers verify part-time lecturers' claims properly payable.	1		
(*c*) Check hours claimed against timetable hours.	1		
(*d*) Check rate of pay agrees with standard of work taught.	1		

Item	*Audit category*	*By (initials)*	*Extent of check (dates, nos., etc.)*
19. *College transport*			
(a) Investigate use of college transport (authority for journeys, recharges where appropriate, log sheets properly kept, continuity of mileage, etc.).	3		
(b) Ensure reasonableness of running costs of vehicle (NB: particularly fuel used).	3		
20. *Financial planning information* Investigate any unusual items or trends of income and expenditure supplied.	2		
Post-audit Carry forward all controlled stationery not cleared at this audit.	1		

APPENDIX 3

Examples of internal control questionnaires

Internal control questionnaire

EXPENDITURE

	Yes	*No*	*Comments*
Obtain the financial regulations regarding expenditure.			
1. *Budget estimates*			
1.1 Do financial regulations provide for the preparation of:			
(*a*) Capital estimates:			
(i) Over a period of more than one year?			
(ii) Over a period of more than three years?			
(*b*) Revenue estimates for more than one year?			
1.2 Is virement allowed? If so:			
(*a*) Is there a procedure specified for its control?			
(*b*) Is there a limit on the amount of virement from any one expenditure head?			
1.3 Do financial regulations provide for:			
(*a*) Application for supplementary estimates? If so:			
(i) Is there a specified procedure?			

	Yes	*No*	*Comments*
(ii) Is there a limit below which committee approval is not required?			
(*b*) An inflation reserve? If so, is there a procedure laid down for the control and allocation of the reserve?			
(c) Specific approval in addition to budget approval for certain categories of expenditure? If so, which expenditure?			
1.4 Do financial regulations specify which categories of revenue expenditure should be subject to the submission of a financial implications report?			
1.5 Is a financial implications report on revenue costs required for proposed capital projects?			
1.6 Is the spending department responsible for budgetary control?			
1.7 Are regular statements of expenditure against estimates supplied to spending departments?			
1.8 Is the chief financial officer responsible for notifying spending departments when: (*a*) Actual expenditure approaches estimate? (*b*) Actual expenditure exceeds estimate? Is action taken at stage (*b*)?			
1.9 Have estimate headings been agreed with the spending departments? If so, are they in the same form as the expenditure analysis headings?			
1.10 Are capital feasibility studies undertaken?			

	Yes	*No*	*Comments*
1.11 Is the chief financial officer responsible for reporting on the cost of capital works? Is the spending department so responsible? At what stage are reports submitted: (*a*) Currently? (*b*) When cost approaches estimate? (*c*) When cost exceeds estimate? (*d*) On completion of works?			
1.12 Are major over/under spendings reported to the committee? If so, is the report submitted by: (*a*) The chief financial officer? (*b*) The spending department?			
1.13 Have the financial regulations been complied with?			
2. *Tenders and quotations* This would be covered in a Contracts ICQ.			
3. *Ordering*			
3.1 Is any distinction drawn between orders for supplies of a routine and recurring nature and orders for supplies of a special and non-recurring nature?			
3.2 Is authority to order restricted to specified officers? If so: (*a*) Is a list of such officers maintained? (*b*) Are orders actually signed by these officers?			
3.3 Are order books controlled?			
3.4 Is the signing officer responsible for receipt or custody of supplies?			
3.5 Are orders supported by a written requisition?			
3.6 Is the requisitioning officer responsible for receipt or custody of supplies?			

	Yes	*No*	*Comments*
3.7 Does the order clearly indicate point of delivery?			
3.8 Does the ordering officer satisfy himself of the necessity for the order?			
3.9 Is a written order sent to the supplier in every case?			
(*a*) Is the form of the order approved by the chief financial officer?			
(*b*) Does the chief financial officer receive a copy of the order? If so:			
(i) Is this at the same time as the orders are despatched to suppliers?			
(ii) Or is the copy order attached to the invoice when submitted for payment?			
(*c*) Does any other person receive a copy of the order?			
3.10 Which officers interview salesmen?			
3.11 Does the department/establishment record commitments against estimates? If so, are financial analysis headings used?			
3.12 Is there a procedure for dealing with verbal orders/emergency orders/open order, etc.? If so, how often is it used?			
3.13 Do order books have a unique prefix or reference which will enable the order to be traced to a department or establishment?			
3.14 Are recommendations on the suitability of firms and their products made available to spending departments and establishments by a central purchasing officer?			

		Yes	No	Comments
	If so, are orders scrutinised to ensure that goods are obtained from recommended sources?			
3.15	Is a time for retention of copy orders specified?			
3.16	Is special attention paid to orders which might cover 'inertia selling' practices, i.e. orders for carbon paper, paint, stock orders, etc.?			
3.17	Are orders 'marked off' when completed?			
4.	*Receipt of goods*			
4.1	Is the receipt of goods authenticated by:			
	(*a*) Receipted delivery notes?			
	(*b*) Signed goods inward sheets?			
	(*c*) Any other method?			
4.2	Are delivery notes or any other stationery recording delivery retained?			
	If so, is a period of retention specified?			
4.3	Are goods checked on delivery as to:			
	(*a*) Quality?			
	(*b*) Quantity?			
4.4	Is there a procedure specified in respect of:			
	(*a*) Rejected deliveries?			
	(*b*) Partial deliveries?			
	(*c*) Over/under deliveries?			
	(*d*) Goods on 'approval'?			
4.5	Are reports submitted to a responsible officer (e.g. central purchasing officer), in respect of:			
	(*a*) Poor quality?			
	(*b*) Delays in deliveries?			
	(*c*) Incomplete deliveries?			
	(*d*) Substitution for 'out of stock' items?			
	If so, is appropriate action taken by him?			

Question	*Yes*	*No*	*Comments*
4.6 Is there adequate security for goods once they have been received?			
4.7 Has someone the sole responsibility for custody and issue of stocks?			
5. *Confirmation of work done*			
Is evidence of satisfactory performance of work done, or services supplied, obtained prior to the relevant invoices being certified?			
6. *Invoice certification and check*			
6.1 Which invoice system is used: (*a*) 'Official'? If so, is it adequately controlled? (*b*) Suppliers?			
6.2 Do financial regulations prescribe the officers authorised to certify invoices? If so: (*a*) Is a current list of signatures maintained? (*b*) Are amendments approved?			
6.3 Are invoices actually certified by these officers?			
6.4 Is the certification by facsimile signature? If so, are the facsimile stamps in safe custody?			
6.5 Does the certifying officer: (*a*) Order supplies? (*b*) Receive supplies?			
6.6 Is there a common invoice grid certification stamp? (i) Is it stamped on the invoice? (ii) Or is it a stick-on certification slip? Does it provide for: (*a*) The reference to specific approval?			

	Yes	*No*	*Comments*
(*b*) That a specific order number is marked off?			
(*c*) That the receipted delivery note or weigh ticket is checked?			
(*d*) That the work is satisfactorily completed?			
(*e*) That prices and discounts are checked?			
(*f*) The minute reference?			
(*g*) That the arithmetic has been checked?			
(*h*) The certification by chief officer?			
(*i*) The expenditure coding and creditor coding?			
(*j*) The reference to inventory or stores ledger?			
(*k*) The examination by the chief financial officer?			
(*l*) That the account has not previously been certified for payment?			
(*m*) The invoice reference?			
(*n*) The VAT allocation?			
6.7 Is there a specified procedure for the payment of copy invoices?			
6.8 Are copy orders endorsed as to the date invoices are submitted to the chief financial officer for payment?			
6.9 Are copy orders marked off on receipt of invoices? If yes, by whom?			
6.10 Does the payments procedure give special treatment to invoices:			
(*a*) Over a certain amount?			
(*b*) Subject to prompt payment discount?			
6.11 Is there a record of recurring payments? If so, is the record held in:			
(*a*) The chief financial officer's department?			

	Yes	No	Comments
(*b*) The spending department?			
(*c*) Both?			
6.12 Is there a procedure for dealing with urgent payments?			
If so, is there machinery for:			
(i) Avoiding duplicate payments?			
(ii) Ensuring that all urgent payments are properly authorised?			
6.13 Are supplier statements examined?			
If so, by whom?			
6.14 Are certified statements refused for payment?			
7. *Analysis of expenditure*			
7.1 Who codes the invoices:			
(*a*) The establishment?			
(*b*) The spending department?			
(*c*) The finance department?			
7.2 If the organisation or spending department is responsible for coding invoices, is the coding checked by the chief financial officer?			
7.3 If the finance department is responsible for coding invoices, is there a separate person responsible for the scrutiny of the coding?			
7.4 Is expenditure analysed by machine process? If so, is the reconciliation of totals the responsibility of someone not involved in the machine process?			
7.5 Is expenditure analysed manually?			
If so, is the reconciliation carried out by someone not involved in the actual analysis?			

	Yes	No	Comments
8. *Outstanding creditors*			
8.1 Do departments prepare lists of outstanding creditors and send them to the chief financial officers: (*a*) At the year end? (*b*) At other times?			
8.2 Are these examined by the chief financial officers?			
9. *General*			
9.1 Do manuals of guidance exist for staff engaged in the payment of invoices in: (*a*) The establishment? (*b*) The spending department? (*c*) The finance department? If so, have they been revised within the last two years?			
9.2 Are the duties of staff separated so that internal check requirements are fulfilled?			
9.3 Are the duties of staff involved in the payment of invoices periodically rotated?			
9.4 Do staff involved in the payment of invoices: (*a*) Take all their leave? (*b*) Complete their duties without working regular overtime?			
9.5 Are staff engaged in the payment of invoices covered by adequate fidelity guarantee insurance?			
9.6 Is there a review procedure for errors located both before and after payment? (*a*) Is the person who performs this review not engaged in the payment of creditors? (*b*) Is a record of errors maintained and periodically examined by a senior member of staff?			

	Yes	No	Comments
(*c*) Are manual alterations allowed for in the system? If so, at what points?			
10. *Travelling expenses and subsistence allowance claims*			
10.1 Are travelling expenses claims: (*a*) Submitted regularly? (*b*) Completed correctly? (*c*) Certified properly?			
10.2 Do departments have satisfactory arrangements for: (*a*) Authorising journeys? (*b*) Checking mileages claimed? (*c*) Ensuring economic use of vehicles?			
10.3 (*a*) Is the cubic capacity of the car shown? (*b*) Has the correct mileage rate been paid?			
10.4 Are the mileages claimed reasonable?			
10.5 Is the purpose of each journey claimed compatible with the individual's post?			
10.6 Is the period of absence from the individual's base sufficient to justify claiming subsistence allowance?			
10.7 Have any passengers shown on the claim also claimed for the same journey?			

Internal control questionnaire

BANK AND CASH TRANSACTIONS

	Yes	*No*	*Comments*
1. *Bank accounts*			
Obtain details of all main and subsidiary bank accounts, with full titles, account numbers and authorised signatories.			
1.1 (*a*) Is there a written statement of bank terms agreed by the organisation's bankers?			
(*b*) Have bank terms been reviewed within a reasonable period (say two to three years)?			
1.2 Are there instructions covering the use and operation of bank accounts in:			
(*a*) The organisation?			
(*b*) The department?			
1.3 Are all these accounts in the name of the organisation?			
1.4 Has the bank been instructed not to open further accounts without proper authority?			
1.5 Do bank terms specify overdraft arrangements on the various accounts?			
1.6 What action has the bank been instructed to take if any subsidiary account becomes overdrawn?			
1.7 Has the bank been instructed on limits (e.g. as to amount payable on one signature) on all accounts?			
1.8 Is money released from the main bank account only to fund subsidiary accounts out of which external payments are made? If so, have instructions been issued covering funding methods?			

	Yes	No	Comments
1.9 If any cheques are drawn on the main account, are there safeguards as to authorisation and signatures?			
1.10 Are there similar safeguards for transfers to subsidiary accounts?			
1.11 Are there safeguards in respect of direct debits?			
1.12 Are there arrangements for controlling 'cash flow'? If so, is a specific officer responsible?			
1.13 Is a responsible officer checking the bank's calculations re.: (*a*) Bank interest? (*b*) Bank charges?			
1.14 Are all subsidiary funds operated on an imprest basis?			
1.15 Are the amounts/existence/needs of the imprests reviewed periodically?			
1.16 Is satisfactory evidence of outgoings produced before the accounts are reimbursed?			
2. *Cheque control*			
2.1 (*a*) Has the person who orders cheques any other part in the payment procedure? (*b*) Is there an indemnity from the printer regarding the fraudulent use of cheques?			
2.2 Are all cheques stored in safe custody?			
2.3 Are all cheque forms issued to approved identified personnel and acknowledged in writing?			
2.4 Is the stock balance of cheque forms verified: (*a*) Daily? (*b*) Weekly?			

	Yes	*No*	*Comments*
2.5 Are 'open' cheques used? If so:			
(*a*) Is there a limit on the amount?			
(*b*) Is their use restricted to specified purposes?			
2.6 Is the number of cheques used reconciled with the number of authorised payments by a person independent of the payments system?			
2.7 (*a*) Are records maintained of spoiled and cancelled cheques?			
(*b*) Are the cheques returned to internal audit?			
2.8 Do cheque writing procedures for normal and urgent payments differ?			
2.9 Where cheques are signed in manuscript:			
(*a*) Are two signatories required?			
(*b*) Is the amount under one signature limited?			
2.10 Where a cheque-signing machine is in use:			
(*a*) Are the key and the dies held by a responsible officer?			
(*b*) Is the number of cheques signed, recorded and agreed with the number of cheques issued?			
(*c*) Is a manuscript initial made on the cheque?			
(*d*) Is such an initial a condition of payment by the bank?			
(*e*) Has the bank accepted instructions to this effect?			
(*f*) Is the amount of any one cheque limited?			

	Yes	*No*	*Comments*
2.11 Where pre-signed cheques are used:			
(*a*) Is a manuscript initial and/or rubber stamp made on the cheque?			
(*b*) Is the authority to do this restricted?			
(*c*) Is this a condition of payment by the bank?			
(*d*) Has the bank accepted instructions to this effect?			
(*e*) Is the amount of any one cheque limited?			
(*f*) Is there a limit above which a manuscript signature is also required?			
(*g*) Is there an indemnity from printers re. misuse?			
2.12 Where signature is by rubber stamp:			
(*a*) Is the stamp holder a responsible officer and does he store the stamp in a secure place?			
(*b*) Is a manuscript initial made on the cheque?			
(*c*) Is such an initial a condition of payment by the bank?			
(*d*) Has the bank accepted instructions to this effect?			
(*e*) Is the amount of any one cheque limited?			
2.13 Is there a procedure for opening crossed cheques?			
(*a*) Is the authority to open cheques restricted to specified officers?			
(*b*) Do instructions specify under what circumstances a cheque can be opened?			
2.14 (*a*) Is there a procedure specified for the preparation of cheques for despatch?			

	Yes	*No*	*Comments*
(*b*) Are all people involved in despatch independent of the payments procedures?			
(*c*) Is a record kept of all cheques not despatched immediately to the creditor?			
(*d*) Is proof of identity and a signature required from creditors who collect their cheques?			
(*e*) Are the cheques kept secure until they are handed to the Post Office?			
2.15 Is there a procedure for handling returned cheques and recording them past the letter opening stage?			
(*a*) Is any independent authority required to authorise the re-issue of cheques?			
2.16 When duplicate cheques are issued, is an indemnity required from the payee?			
2.17 Is there a facility to stop cheques? If so, is it controlled?			
2.18 Are alterations to cheques permitted? If so, are they controlled?			
2.19 Is a fidelity guarantee in force with adequate cover for defalcations concerning cheques?			
3. *Reconciliation*			
Do reconciliation procedures provide for:			
3.1 The designation of an officer responsible for bank reconciliation? If so, is he independent of preparation and despatch of cheques?			
3.2 A set frequency for obtaining paid cheques from the bank?			

		Yes	No	Comments
3.3	The intervals at which reconciliations must be effected?			
3.4	The requirements concerning authorisation for writing back unpresented cheques?			
3.5	The reconciliation of payments with expenditure analysis?			
3.6	A procedure to be followed in the event of errors arising?			
4.	*Petty cash, postage and minor disbursement accounts*			
	Obtain details of all accounts which are in existence.			
4.1	Do regulations provide that persons responsible for operating accounts are individually specified by name and post and notified to the chief financial officer?			
4.2	Are accounts which must be kept on an imprest basis specified?			
4.3	Are payments restricted to account holders only?			
4.4	Is there a limit on the amount of any one payment?			
4.5	Are account holders personally responsible for custody of cash (stamps)?			
4.6	Must bank accounts be opened when the amount held is over defined limits?			
4.7	Is access to cash (stamps) limited to account holders?			
4.8	Are overdrafts on bank accounts prohibited?			
4.9	Are advances/reimbursements made only on receipt of supporting evidence?			
4.10	Are acknowledgements from account holders required at specific intervals?			

	Yes	*No*	*Comments*
4.11 Are cash balances checked periodically by persons other than account holders? If so, are balances and dates recorded?			
4.12 Are any accounts funded by round sum advances? If so, are there rules governing the authorisation and control of such advances?			
4.13 Has an officer been designated as being responsible for determining the total advance to be held by each individual account holder?			

Internal control questionnaire

STORES AND STOCKTAKING

Statistics

Period	No. of receipts	No. of issues	Stock at		Annual turnover £
			No. of items	Value £	

	Name(s)	Location
Storekeeper(s).		
Officer with overall control of stores system.		
Officer responsible for stocktaking.		
Accounting records kept by:		
Bin card.		
Stores ledger – manual.		
Stores ledger – mechanical.		
Issue transfer and return notes.		
Goods received notes.		
Stock adjustment notes.		
Order books.		
Copy orders.		
Invoices.		
Computer.		

	Method	Date last completed
Stocktaking procedure.		
Stock valuation basis.		

	Yes	*No*	*Comments*
1. *Security*			
1.1 Was auditor asked to show any identification prior to access?			
1.2 Is there a controlled access point?			
1.3 Do premises appear secure against intruders?			
1.4 Can storekeepers observe all exits? If 'no', is any improvement possible?			
1.5 Is the storekeeper the only key holder? (If 'no', list other keyholders.) Are the keys kept in a safe place?			
1.6 Is the storekeeper the only person allowed to receive and issue stores? If 'no', give details.			
1.7 Is there adequate control of the goods inwards bay in order to prevent pilfering by visiting delivery people?			
1.8 Is it possible for unauthorised persons to collect goods from the dispatch bay?			
1.9 Can control of either bay be improved? If 'yes', give details.			
1.10 Is the store and its contents adequately insured for loss?			
2. *Fuel*			
2.1 Does the storekeeper control vehicle fuel stocks?			
2.2 Are fuel pumps and inlets locked when not in use?			
2.3 Do drivers sign for fuel issues?			
2.4 Are vehicle registration numbers recorded on the issue sheets?			
2.5 Are fuel pump meter readings recorded on issue sheets?			
2.6 When were pumps last checked for accuracy of quantity delivered and recorded?			

	Yes	No	Comments
2.7 Is dipping done at regular intervals by a person other than the storekeeper?			
2.8 Are tolerance levels allowed? If 'yes', specify.			
2.9 Are statistics of level of issues prepared?			
2.10 Do these show the trend of issues you would expect? Is this reviewed regularly?			
2.11 Are there adequate arrangements for recharging other authorised users?			
3. *Ordering*			
3.1 Are official orders used for stores items in all cases?			
3.2 Are verbal orders permitted in an emergency only? Does the system ensure that written confirmation follows by next working day?			
3.3 Is the person signing orders: (*a*) Authorised to do so? (*b*) Independent of the storekeeper?			
3.4 Does the storekeeper initiate requisitions for orders?			
3.5 Does the storekeeper get a copy of the order?			
3.6 Are orders issued only to approved suppliers, in accordance with buying policy?			
3.7 Are they within any authorised limits laid down by the organisation?			
3.8 Are the net prices obtained, the lowest possible? If 'no', give any other deciding factors (i.e. delivery date, etc.).			
3.9 How often are suppliers asked to tender?			
3.10 Who interviews salesmen wishing to supply stock items?			

	Yes	No	Comments
3.11 Are maximum/re-order/ minimum levels of stock laid down?			
3.12 Are these levels regularly reviewed?			
4. *Receipts*			
4.1 Are all deliveries checked, before acceptance, to: (*a*) Delivery notes? (*b*) Copy orders? If 'no', is the delivery note marked to show 'subject to a detailed check'?			
4.2 Are all bulk materials weighed before being accepted, or is an official weigh ticket produced?			
4.3 Is the system for part deliveries adequate?			
4.4 Are goods received notes prepared?			
4.5 Are all goods received promptly recorded and taken into store?			
4.6 Is the recording of goods received independent of the checking of invoices?			
4.7 Is the person certifying the invoice as to goods received: (*a*) Authorised to do so? (*b*) Independent of the storekeeper?			
4.8 Are there adequate procedures to ensure: (*a*) Return of goods to suppliers? (*b*) Claims for shortages, breakages and incorrect deliveries? (*c*) All credit notes received? (*d*) Return and control of chargeable containers, etc.?			
5. *Issues*			
5.1 Are requisitions/issue notes completed for all issues being made?			

	Yes	*No*	*Comments*
5.2 Are requisitions/issue notes correctly made out and authorised by persons who are not storekeepers?			
5.3 Are requisitions/issue notes examined for reasonableness of quantities? If so: (*a*) By whom? (*b*) At what stage?			
5.4 Is there a list of persons who are authorised to sign requisitions/ issue notes?			
5.5 Does the storekeeper know who is authorised to sign requisitions/ issue notes?			
5.6 Does the recipient sign for all items received?			
5.7 Are all bulk materials weighed before issue?			
5.8 Are the procedures in respect of unfulfilled requisitions/issue notes satisfactory?			
5.9 Are arrangements for 'emergency' or 'night shift' issues adequate?			
6. *Returns/transfers*			
6.1 Are goods returned notes used for: (*a*) Unused items? (*b*) Second-hand items? (*c*) Scrap?			
6.2 Does the person who authorises the issues make out a goods returned note? If 'no', detail.			
6.3 Does the storekeeper acknowledge the receipt of items returned?			
6.4 Are second-hand stores kept separate from new items?			
6.5 Are transfers between stores properly documented?			

	Yes	*No*	*Comments*
6.6 Are goods returned promptly recorded and taken into store?			
6.7 Is the level of returns unduly high?			
7. *Sales*			
7.1 Are sales allowed?			
7.2 Are sales restricted to particular items? If 'yes', specify.			
7.3 Are sales restricted to certain categories of persons? If so, are sales made only to these categories of person?			
7.4 Are the sales properly documented?			
7.5 (*a*) Is the authority's policy of charging being adhered to?			
(*b*) Are sales prices adequate to ensure no financial loss to the organisation?			
7.6 Are competitive tenders invited for the sale of scrap?			
7.7 Is cash received/sale authorised by a person independent of the storekeeper?			
7.8 Does the storekeeper ensure that the payment is received and the sale authorised before goods are issued?			
8. *Accounting records*			
8.1 Where stores records are posted from prime documents, are there arrangements to ensure that all such documents are accounted for?			
8.2 Is the ledger updated at intervals not greater than those specified by management?			
8.3 Are adequate measures taken to ensure that the ledger shows an up-to-date position?			

	Yes	*No*	*Comments*
8.4 Are the procedures for dealing with the following satisfactory from the point of view of authorisation and correct recording? (*a*) Additional new stock items (including allocation of commodity codes). (*b*) Deletion of stock items. And, where applicable: (*c*) Adjustment of prices. (*d*) Adjustment of unit of issue. (*e*) Adjustment of minimum or maximum stock levels. (*f*) Adjustment of re-order quantities.			
8.5 (*a*) Are items of small value treated as consumable? (*b*) Is a list kept of these items? (*c*) Is this list reviewed at regular intervals?			
8.6 Is there any duplication of manual and computer records? If 'yes', give details.			
9. *Stocktaking*			
9.1 Is stocktaking carried out independently of the storekeeper/stores control check?			
9.2 Are all stock checks supported by stock taking sheets? If 'yes', are stocks checked: (*a*) Continuously? (*b*) At set intervals?			
9.3 Are all items checked at least once every year?			
9.4 (*a*) Are attractive and valuable items checked at least monthly? (*b*) Is the level of shortages in this area high, either in number or value?			
9.5 Are all discrepancies investigated and reported on? If so, by whom?			

		Yes	*No*	*Comments*
9.6	Are all write-offs properly authorised?			
9.7	(*a*) Is the ledger adjusted for discrepancies immediately the authority to do so is given?			
	(*b*) Is the control of the disposal of obsolete items adequate?			
	(*c*) Are tenders invited in appropriate cases for the disposal of such items?			
10.	*Management information*			
10.1	Does the system provide for, *inter alia*:			
	(*a*) Information on slow moving/ obsolete items at regular intervals?			
	(*b*) Review of maximum/ minimum levels and re-order levels?			
	(*c*) Details of stock levels held on comparative dates?			
10.2	Is appropriate action taken on management information produced?			
10.3	(*a*) Does a procedure manual exist?			
	(*b*) Have all the staff concerned got copies?			
	(*c*) When was it last reviewed?			
11.	*Inventories*			
11.1	Is an inventory kept? If so, has the head of the establishment a copy of the instructions regarding inventories?			
11.2	Has a stock check of equipment been carried out within the last 12 months? If so:			
	(*a*) By whom?			
	(*b*) Is there satisfactory evidence of this?			

	Yes	*No*	*Comments*
11.3 Have recently purchased articles been entered in the inventory?			
11.4 Are serial numbers and/or types of relatively valuable articles entered in the inventory?			
11.5 (*a*) Has a list been kept of the number and value of trophies/cups?			
(*b*) Are they covered by insurance?			
11.6 Have details of gifts been reported to managers/governors and recorded on the inventory?			
11.7 Are there any items which the head of the organisation regards as surplus to requirements?			
11.8 Has any income arisen from write-offs and disposals and has it been brought into account?			
11.9 Have all write-offs been properly authorised?			
11.10 Is any form of identification marking (e.g. identification paint) used? If so, has it been applied to all relevant items?			
11.11 Is a copy of the inventory held elsewhere?			

General comments regarding the system

1. Do you consider:
   (*a*) The store is necessary?
   (*b*) The store is cost effective?
   (*c*) The store is correctly located?
   (*d*) The general layout and operation of the store to be efficient?
   (*e*) The number of staff to be too high/too low/correct?
   (*f*) The general competence of the staff to be high/low/adequate?
2. Any other comments.

Internal control questionnaire

CONTROL OF INCOME

	Yes	No	Comments
1. *Postal remittances*			
1.1 Are remittances ever received by post? If 'yes':			
1.2 Is post received through a post box?			
1.3 If post box is used, is it locked? If so, does it have two locks operated by different keys?			
1.4 Are keys to the post box properly controlled in that they are held by separate people?			
1.5 (*a*) Does more than one person clear the post box?			
(*b*) Is the mail delivered directly and quickly to the post openers?			
1.6 Can the contents be removed from the post box by un-authorised persons? (In other words, is the aperture too large and is the lock adequate?)			
1.7 Can the post box be removed complete with contents?			
1.8 If a post box is not used:			
(*a*) How is the post received?			
(*b*) By whom is it received?			
(*c*) Is the post opened immediately?			
(*d*) If not, is it kept securely?			
1.9 Does more than one person open the post?			
1.10 Who supervises the post opening procedure?			
1.11 Does the cashier assist in the opening of post?			
1.12 Do postal remittances consist of:			
(*a*) Cheques, MOs, POs?			
(*b*) Cash?			

	Yes	*No*	*Comments*
1.13 Are all remittances other than cash immediately crossed to the bank account by the post opening staff?			
1.14 Are all remittances recorded immediately in a remittance record, giving details of payer, amount paid and type of remittance? If not, are cash remittances recorded?			
1.15 At what time are remittance records prepared?			
1.16 Does the supervisor sign these records?			
1.17 Are remittance records totalled and agreed with remittances before they leave the section where the post is opened?			
1.18 Once the post has been opened, are all remittances immediately handed to:			
(*a*) The cashier?			
(*b*) Other departments as appropriate?			
(*c*) Any other person?			
1.19 Are discharges received?			
1.20 Is a satisfactory system in operation for dealing with post-dated or incorrectly made out cheques, or misaddressed remittances?			
1.21 Are receipts issued for:			
(*a*) All postal remittances including cheques?			
(*b*) Cheques on request only?			
1.22 If yes, are these issued:			
(*a*) By the staff opening the post, when it is opened?			
(*b*) At a later stage?			
1.23 Is there a procedure for dealing with unidentified remittances? If so:			
(*a*) Is the system satisfactory?			

	Yes	*No*	*Comments*
(*b*) Are appropriate steps taken to identify such remittances?			
1.24 Are receipts agreed to remittance records: (*a*) In total? (*b*) Individually? If so, by whom?			
1.25 Is all recorded and registered mail signed for by a senior assistant and recorded in a registered post book? If so: (*a*) Are the packets opened under supervision? (*b*) Are the contents entered into the registered post book?			
1.26 If the answer to para. 1.25 is 'no', how is the registered and recorded mail dealt with?			
1.27 Are all the remittances received during the day, which do not require a receipt, placed in a suitably marked receptacle by the payer? If 'yes': (*a*) Is this opened by more than one person? (*b*) Are such remittances dealt with by the normal post opening system?			
1.28 If the answer to para. 1.27 is 'no', how are remittances received during the day, which do not require a receipt, dealt with?			
1.29 Does anyone associated with the receipt of income handle accountancy records?			
2. *Remittances received by staff*			
2.1 (*a*) Which staff, other than cashiers, receive remittances? (*b*) Is this in the normal course of their duty?			

	Yes	No	Comments
(*c*) If not, how often do they receive remittances and why?			
2.2 Do these staff:			
(*a*) Issue official receipts?			
(*b*) Keep a record of all remittances received?			
(*c*) Remit at regular intervals?			
(*d*) Remit cash intact?			
2.3 Are the staff's records reconciled with paying-in records?			
2.4 By whom?			
2.5 Are issues of paying-in books controlled?			
2.6 Security of cash – see Section 13.			
2.7 Are official sums banked/paid to the finance department:			
(*a*) Weekly?			
(*b*) More than once a week?			
(*c*) Less than once a week?			
If (*c*), are the reasons for this satisfactory?			
2.8 Who normally visits the bank/finance department to pay in money?			
(*a*) Are routes and times regularly varied?			
(*b*) Is an escort provided?			
2.9 Is a maximum sum for overnight retention fixed for each collecting employee?			
2.10 Does the person in charge know of the insurance position regarding:			
(*a*) Cash in transit?			
(*b*) The use of private cars by members of staff on official business?			
3. *Receipting systems*			
3.1 Are all remittances receipted? If not, specify reasons.			
3.2 What method of receipting is employed:			
(*a*) Manually written receipts with carbon copy?			

	Yes	No	Comments
(b) Manually written receipts without carbon copy?			
(c) Cash registers or receipting machines?			
(d) Visual display units?			
(e) Sales notes, tickets or similiar documents?			
(f) Other means? (Specify details.)			
3.3 Are manually produced receipts made out in ink?			
3.4 Does the person who receives the money, sign or initial in his own name?			
3.5 Are carbon copies kept? If so:			
(a) How many?			
(b) By whom are they kept?			
3.6 Are all copies of cancelled receipts retained? If so:			
(a) Who retains them?			
(b) Is there a procedure for their eventual destruction?			
3.7 Is all receipting stationery controlled by a section independent of the cashier's section?			
4. *Cash registers and receipting machines*			
4.1 Give details of make and number of each cash register or receipting machine in use at this location.			
4.2 Are till roll totals reconciled daily to cash takings and recorded in a permanent register?			
4.3 (a) Are dates and reset numbers recorded on the till rolls at the end of each day's operations? If so, by whom?			

		Yes	*No*	*Comments*
	(*b*) Is this operation carried out by a person independently of the machine operator? If so, by whom?			
4.4	Is access to the register reset operation and till roll restricted? If so:			
	(*a*) Is it restricted to the person who carries out the operation in para. 4.3?			
	(*b*) Does he/she retain the key?			
4.5	Are old till rolls retained for inspection?			
4.6	For how long are they retained?			
4.7	Are the keys to the machine properly controlled?			
4.8	How many cashiers can use each machine?			
4.9	Can each cashier's takings be reconciled separately? If so, is there a system for overs and unders?			
4.10	Are details of the amount paid visible to the payer?			
4.11	Does the person paying receive a receipt or other form of acknowledgement?			
4.12	Are any other receptacles used to collect and hold cash?			
4.13	What records are kept of cash registers or receipting machines:			
	(*a*) In use?			
	(*b*) In reserve?			
4.14	Is any analysis of income produced by the machine?			
4.15	If so, in what form?			
5.	*Collectors' registers (e.g. rent collectors)*			
5.1	Are any monies collected by means of collectors' registers? If so, specify.			
5.2	Are stocks of stationery adequately controlled?			

	Yes	*No*	*Comments*
5.3 Are the main accounting records maintained independently from the collector?			
5.4 Are independent checks carried out to ensure that prime records held by debtors agree with official records?			
6. *Income where no receipt is given (e.g. confectionery sales and coin boxes)*			
6.1 Is cash collected from coin boxes (e.g. telephones, hair-dryers and games):			
(*a*) Regularly?			
(*b*) By two people, if there is no meter?			
(*c*) Paid over to the cashier?			
(*d*) Subsequently compared with expenditure on the equipment?			
6.2 Is an adequate record of the takings kept?			
6.3 Is the cash paid over regularly?			
If applicable:			
6.4 Are regular stock checks carried out by an independent person?			
6.5 Is income regularly evaluated from stock records, invoices, etc., and reconciled to expenditure?			
6.6 Are profit ratios examined critically at regular intervals in order to establish whether a satisfactory return is being obtained?			
7. *Tickets*			
7.1 For what purpose are tickets used?			
7.2 (*a*) Are the tickets pre-numbered for each purpose?			
(*b*) Is a register kept of their issue?			

	Yes	*No*	*Comments*
7.3 How are tickets issued: (*a*) By machine? If 'yes', specify. (*b*) By hand? If 'yes', by whom?			
7.4 Are tickets surrendered by the purchaser to a second officer?			
7.5 If so, to whom?			
7.6 Are tickets: (*a*) Cancelled and clipped? (*b*) Collected intact?			
7.7 If collected intact, are they destroyed properly by a senior officer?			
7.8 If a collecting ticket box is used, is it properly locked and controlled?			
7.9 Are regular ticket inspections made?			
7.10 If so, how frequently and by whom?			
7.11 Are the tickets, etc., sold reconciled to the cash taken daily?			
7.12 If so, by whom?			
7.13 Is he independent of the person issuing the tickets?			
7.14 Is a periodical reconciliation of the tickets, etc., issued to the establishment carried out?			
7.15 By whom, and how does he evidence it?			
7.16 Are prices shown on tickets?			
7.17 If not: (*a*) Is the description wording both clear and adequate? (*b*) Are signboards satisfactorily worded and sited?			
7.18 Are there adequate storage facilities for tickets?			
8. *Sales notes*			
8.1 For what purpose are sales notes issued?			

	Yes	*No*	*Comments*
8.2 (*a*) Are they pre-numbered for each purpose?			
(*b*) Is a register kept of their issue?			
8.3 (*a*) How many copies are produced?			
(*b*) How many copies are handed to the purchaser?			
(*c*) How many copies are retained?			
8.4 Are the goods to be purchased collected at another point? If so:			
(*a*) How many copies of the sales note are relinquished by the purchaser?			
(*b*) Is at least one copy retained by the person who issued it?			
(*c*) Is the transfer of the goods acknowledged by the signature of the purchaser on the retained copy?			
(*d*) Are stock records properly maintained?			
(*e*) Are retained copies of the sales note properly filed?			
8.5 If the answer to para. 8.4 is 'no', detail the system for the collection of goods and check the procedures.			
9. *Visual display units* This would be dealt with in a Computer ICQ.			
10. *Other means of receipting*			
10.1 Give details of any other means of receipting.			
10.2 Is the internal check adequate?			
11. *Payments to bank*			
11.1 Are there instructions for the banking of income?			
11.2 When are each day's takings banked?			
11.3 Is all cash banked intact?			

		Yes	*No*	*Comments*
11.4	Is the cash received used to make payments?			
11.5	Is the preparation of the paying-in slip and the payment into the bank carried out with adequate separation of duties?			
11.6	(*a*) Are all cheques banked in the next possible banking?			
	(*b*) Is the name of the establishment marked on the back of each cheque?			
	(*c*) Does the recording conform to the requirements of the Accounts and Audit Regulations (e.g. the cheques listed on the paying-in slip are referenced to receipt numbers)?			
11.7	Is the total of all income received at the establishment reconciled to bankings in a satisfactory record (e.g. a C & D book)?			
11.8	Are collections checked against the bank statement by persons independent from those involved in para. 11.5 above?			
11.9	Are cheques not accepted by the bank, recorded and controlled upon their return to the organisation?			
11.10	(*a*) Who has authority to instruct the bank to make adjustments between accounts?			
	(*b*) Is this satisfactory?			
12.	*Cashier*			
12.1	Does the cashier have other cash-handling responsibilities? If so, specify.			
12.2	Does the cashier have access to ledgers, accounts or write-offs?			
12.3	(*a*) To whom does the cashier report any deficiencies?			

	Yes	No	Comments
(*b*) Are they investigated immediately and properly recorded?			
12.4 Has each cashier a separate till, and does he balance it separately?			
12.5 Is the cashier responsible for processing bank credits?			
12.6 Are satisfactory arrangements in operation to cover any absence of the cashier, including holidays?			
13. *Security*			
13.1 Is cash retained in the office overnight?			
13.2 Is the amount held overnight kept to a minimum?			
13.3 (*a*) What type and make(s) of safe does the organisation have?			
(*b*) Is the safe properly anchored or installed?			
(*c*) Is it of adequate strength and size?			
(*d*) Does it conform to insurance requirements?			
13.4 (*a*) Who holds the safe keys?			
(*b*) Are they held by him/her personally?			
(*c*) Who has knowledge of the combination lock numbers?			
(*d*) Is the combination number written down anywhere?			
(*e*) Has a copy of the combination numbers been deposited with a bank under security arrangements?			
(*f*) Is the combination number changed at least once per annum?			

No.	Question	*Yes*	*No*	*Comments*
	(*g*) Is the combination number changed after a member of staff with knowledge of the number leaves his/her employment?			
13.5	(*a*) Is the person in charge aware of the limit of cash to be held overnight on the premises?			
	(*b*) Are all official monies held in the safe overnight?			
	(*c*) Is the person in charge aware of the insurance position relating to cash held on the premises?			
	(*d*) Are unofficial or voluntary funds also held in the safe?			
	(*e*) If so, does this affect the insurance position relating to official monics?			
13.6	(*a*) Is all official money held securely, prior to its being handed to the administrative staff or cashier?			
	(*b*) Are all sums collected handed to the administrative staff or cashier the same day?			
	(*c*) Is a receipt given by the cashier or administrative staff for all collections handed to them by other staff?			
13.7	Is the person in charge aware of the steps to be taken in the event of a burglary?			
13.8	Is the person in charge aware of the procedure for notifying internal audit of a suspected irregularity?			
13.9	Does the cash office provide sufficient protection to staff by means of:			
	(*a*) Counter grilles?			
	(*b*) Lack of access to public?			
	(*c*) Lockable tills?			
	(*d*) Alarm systems?			

	Yes	*No*	*Comments*
(*e*) Any other provisions? (Specify.)			
13.10 Is the insurance cover adequate?			
13.11 Do arrangements for transporting money comply with the insurance cover?			
14. *Income due*			
CALCULATION OF CHARGES			
14.1 Specify which types of income arise in the department/location.			
14.2 Is the basis of charge fixed by reference to:			
(*a*) A statutory decision?			
(*b*) A committee decision?			
(*c*) A decision by a senior member of staff?			
(*d*) The cost of providing the services?			
(*e*) Any other means? (Specify.)			
14.3 If the amount receivable is calculated in accordance with a scale of charges, has the scale been reviewed recently? Specify:			
(*a*) Minute number.			
(*b*) Operative date.			
(*c*) Any other authorisation. (Attach copy of current scale.)			
14.4 If the amount receivable is calculated by reference to personal means, is this in accordance with the basic scheme of assessment and has this scheme been reviewed recently? Specify:			
(*a*) Minute number.			
(*b*) Operative date.			
14.5 Are assessments checked by another member of staff?			
14.6 Are personal circumstances regularly reviewed?			

	Yes	*No*	*Comments*
14.7 (*a*) Who is responsible for initiating a review of the scales of charges?			
(*b*) When were they last reviewed?			
14.8 Are revisions to scales of charges implemented promptly?			
14.9 If the scale is designed to recoup the full cost or a specified proportion of the cost, is the policy regarding this being adhered to?			
14.10 Who is responsible for implementation of revised scales of charges once they have been approved?			
CREDIT INCOME			
14.11 Could the income be collected on a prepayment basis before or at the same time the service was rendered?			
14.12 Is there a satisfactory system to ensure that all credit transactions are recorded and dealt with properly:			
(*a*) For services rendered?			
(*b*) For agreements?			
(*c*) For specially minuted items?			
(*d*) For other items?			
14.13 Is there an adequate record to ensure that periodic or recurring charges are made?			
(*a*) What form does this record take?			
(*b*) Who is responsible for keeping this record?			
14.14 Are debits set up to control income due?			
14.15 Is this work done by:			
(*a*) A debtor's account?			
(*b*) An entry in an accounting record?			
(*c*) Any other means? (Specify.)			

	Yes	*No*	*Comments*
14.16 Are debtors' accounts prepared:			
(*a*) Promptly?			
(*b*) By the department concerned?			
(*c*) By the financial services department?			
(*d*) In numerical sequence?			
(*e*) To include the code to be credited?			
(*f*) To show the amount of VAT included?			
(*g*) To show the discounts allowed?			
14.17 Is the supply of debtors' accounts controlled by a department or section independent of the one raising the debit?			
14.18 How many copies of each debtor's account are prepared?			
14.19 (*a*) What is the document flow in relation to each copy?			
(*b*) If applicable, is the Treasurer's copy forwarded promptly?			
(*c*) If a copy is held at the establishment, are all payments recorded on it?			
14.20 (*a*) Are copy accounts retained for the period required for such documents?			
(*b*) In what order are they filed?			
14.21 Are debtors directed to make payments to:			
(*a*) The financial services department?			
(*b*) The department providing the service?			
(*c*) Any other location?			
14.22 Is there proper control over:			
(*a*) The cancellation of accounts?			
(*b*) The alteration of accounts?			
(*c*) The issue of credit notes?			
14.23 Is the necessary follow up action for recovery clearly laid down, and is it observed?			

	Yes	No	Comments
14.24 Where debtors pay accounts at the establishment, is the procedure for notification of overdue accounts to the Treasurer being adhered to?			
14.25 Is the financial services department responsible for the recovery of outstanding debts?			
14.26 Is the service-providing department involved at any stage in the recovery procedure? If so, specify.			
14.27 Are amendments to debits approved at a suitable senior level and in accordance with the laid-down procedure?			
14.28 Is the procedure laid down by the organisation for writing off of debts being adhered to?			
14.29 What are the provisions for writing off outstanding amounts or amending debits?			
14.30 Is there a separation of duties between the person rendering an account and those concerned with receiving the cash?			
14.31 How are sums handled which are not due to the authority?			
14.32 Is there an undue delay in the receipt of income in comparison with the earliest date it could have been received?			
14.33 (*a*) Is a list of bad debtors maintained to whom supplies and services will not be supplied?			
(*b*) Is it implemented?			
15. *Income estimates*			
15.1 Are income estimates prepared:			
(*a*) By heads of departments?			
(*b*) In conjunction with heads of departments?			

	Yes	No	Comments
15.2 Are these estimates in the same form as income analysis headings?			
15.3 Does the chief financial officer notify heads of departments of variations from estimates. If so: (*a*) Is this done by way of: (i) An exception report? (ii) Otherwise? (*b*) At what intervals?			
15.4 Are variations from estimates promptly investigated?			
15.5 Are variations required to be reported to committee? If so, in what circumstances?			
16. *Unofficial/voluntary funds*			
16.1 Are the organisation's unofficial funds regulations operated?			
16.2 (*a*) Are the accounts audited by the internal audit section? (*b*) If not, are they audited by a person with relevant qualifications as required by the organisation's policy?			
16.3 Is an annual financial statement and audit certificate submitted to the management committee/managers/governors in respect of each fund maintained?			
If internal audit is responsible for the audit of unofficial funds, the following questions should be asked:			
16.4 Are at least two persons required to sign cheques on all funds?			
16.5 With trading activities (e.g. school tuckshop) are the records maintained sufficient to enable profit margins to be calculated?			

	Yes	*No*	*Comments*
16.6 Where outgoings and visits are supported from unofficial funds, are detailed statements of receipts and payments prepared and signed by the teacher/person responsible?			
16.7 Are receipts issued to parents who make contributions in respect of such visits?			

APPENDIX 4

Internal control questionnaire on the adequacy of internal audit

Internal control questionnaire

ADEQUACY OF INTERNAL AUDIT

The purpose of this questionnaire is to assist in determining the adequacy and effectiveness of internal audit arrangements within an organisation. External auditors will find it useful for this purpose and it will also assist directors of finance, chief internal auditors and others to assess their own arrangements for internal audit.

	Yes	*No*	*Comments*
1. *Role and objectives*			
1.1 Have the responsibilities of the internal audit division/section been properly determined and set out formally?			
1.2 Is it the responsibility of internal audit to review, appraise and report upon:			
(*a*) The soundness, adequacy and application of financial and other management controls.			
(*b*) The extent of compliance with, relevance and financial effect of, established policies, plans and procedures?			

	Yes	*No*	*Comments*
(*c*) The extent to which the organisation's assets and interests are accounted for and safeguarded from losses of all kinds arising from:			
(i) Fraud and other offences?			
(ii) Waste, extravagance and inefficient administration, poor value-for-money or other cause?			
(*d*) The suitability and reliability of financial and other management data developed within the organisation, as specified in the CIPFA statement on internal audit?			
1.3 Does the division/section operate independently of line management?			
1.4 Is audit activity restricted by management policy to the detriment of audit's effectiveness?			
1.5 Does the chief internal auditor have direct access, if necessary, to the director of finance, the chief executive, or other senior employees?			
1.6 Is the division/section free of any obligation to undertake duties within the organisation other than audit?			
1.7 Is there a satisfactory working relationship with O & M and other management services sections which ensures the maximum overall effectiveness of the sections and that there is no unnecessary duplication of effort?			
2. *Liaison with external audit*			
2.1 Are regular meetings held with external auditors?			

	Yes	No	Comments
2.2 Is the audit plan (see question 5.2) co-ordinated with the external auditors in order that unnecessary duplication of work can be avoided?			
2.3 Is there an interchange of all reports issued by both internal and external audit?			
2.4 Has it been agreed that the chief internal auditor will notify external audit at an early stage of any significant fraud or loss?			
3. *Organisation and staffing*			
Obtain and attach an organisational chart for the audit division/section, together with a statement of strength, divided up between qualified, non-qualified and clerical staff.			
3.1 Is the overall strength of the division/section considered to be adequate in relation to the size and type of organisation?			
3.2 Is the head of internal audit a professionally qualified and experienced auditor?			
3.3 Is the proportion of professionally qualified and experienced staff considered adequate?			
3.4 Is there an adequate number of specialist staff experienced in such matters as computer processing, contracts, investments, etc.?			
3.5 Is there a properly defined division of staff into sections covering different services or departments, each under the control of an experienced team leader?			
3.6 Are opportunities provided for regular exchanges of views and information between team leaders and senior auditors?			

	Yes	No	Comments
3.7 Have job specifications been prepared which define the duties of all senior members of the audit division/section?			
4. *Training arrangements*			
4.1 Is there a designated audit training officer?			
4.2 Is there an in-service training programme and, if so, is the syllabus considered adequate?			
4.3 Are all new and inexperienced staff members expected to participate in the programme?			
4.4 Is there provision for members of staff to undertake external courses and is the method of selection for these courses considered satisfactory?			
4.5 Is a training record maintained for each student which records courses and lectures attended, examinations passed, practical experience acquired, etc.?			
4.6 Is there a feed-back on courses from students to enable the effectiveness and relevance of subjects to be assessed?			
4.7 Are trainees and students given the opportunity to participate actively in all types of audit and to undertake practical work, such as the drafting of reports, preparation of audit programmes, flow charts, etc.?			
5. *Planning and control of audits*			
5.1 Is there a long-term plan designed to ensure that all objectives are attained over a period?			

		Yes	No	Comments
5.2	Is an annual plan, based on the resources available, prepared in accordance with the requirements of the long-term plan? (See also question 2.2.)			
5.3	Is this plan considered to give an adequate cover, particularly in high risk areas?			
5.4	Is any formal system of risk analysis employed to establish these areas of risk?			
5.5	Is progress against the annual plan monitored at regular intervals and reported to the director of finance?			
5.6	Is audit time recorded and analysed to show how audit resources have been employed and to enable comparison with targets to be effected?			
6.	*Quality control of audits*			
6.1	Are planned visits made routinely by senior staff to auditors in the field to carry out on-the-spot inspections of work being carried out?			
6.2	Are in-depth checks carried out by senior staff from time to time on completed files and working papers, in order to assess the quality of the work carried out?			
6.3	Is any other system of quality control of audits in force?			
7.	*Conduct of audits*			
7.1	Have audit programmes been prepared in respect of each service or department subject to audit and are these programmes considered adequate?			

	Yes	*No*	*Comments*
7.2 Are adequate audit files maintained for each service or department audited which contain details such as the staff organisation, flow charts, audit programme, working papers and correspondence relating to previous audits, etc.?			
7.3 Are files reviewed by senior staff on a planned basis in order to ensure that the audit programmes in use remain relevant to current systems and that other information is up to date?			
7.4 Before an audit is undertaken, are the audit staff concerned properly briefed by the team leader and are instructions given which detail the sections of the audit programme to be covered, any potential weaknesses that may exist and any aspects that may require special investigation?			
7.5 Are systems in operation documented on audit files and are audit staff required to update this information on each audit visit?			
7.6 Are adequate audit working papers maintained for each audit so that the extent of audit work carried out can be established, the conclusion (drawn by the auditor from tests carried out) shown and any information relating to the audit readily obtained?			
7.7 Is audit work not carried out for any particular reason noted for follow up later?			

	Yes	No	Comments
7.8 Are there standing instructions to audit staff that, if they become aware of a serious breakdown of control, this should be reported at once to the head of the division/section?			
7.9 Are there standing instructions to the chief internal auditor to make an immediate review when such a situation is reported and to report to the director of finance and/or the chief executive in order that corrective action can be taken?			
7.10 Which aspects of the computer are reviewed by audit staff:			
(*a*) The purchase of equipment?			
(*b*) System development? (This includes feasibility studies, system specifications and system testing and implementation.)			
(*c*) Standards? (This includes the rules and procedures for project control, system design and programming and operations.)			
(*d*) Computer operations and/or control section?			
(*e*) Financial post-implementation review?			
8. *Audit reports*			
8.1 Is a satisfactory form of audit report in use for the reporting of audit findings, system weaknesses, control failures, losses or irregularities and for the submission of recommendations to management?			

	Yes	No	Comments
8.2 Are the proposed findings and recommendations discussed with the head of department concerned (or with a level of employee accepted by the departmental head) before the conclusion of the audit?			
8.3 Are completed audit reports reviewed by team leaders and the chief internal auditor before being submitted to management?			
8.4 Are all reports issued countersigned by the chief internal auditor?			
8.5 Does the chief internal auditor report to the highest level of management within the organisation:			
(*a*) In all cases?			
(*b*) Only in cases where the director of finance is personally involved?			
8.6 Is there a satisfactory system of follow up on recommendations made to ensure that appropriate action is taken?			
9. *Audit techniques in use*			
9.1 Is use made, in appropriate cases, of the following techniques:			
(*a*) Flow charting?			
(*b*) Internal control questionnaires?			
(*c*) Computer – interrogation or computer test packs?			
(*d*) Statistical sampling?			

APPENDIX 5

External audit questionnaire on internal audit practice

External audit questionnaire

INTERNAL AUDIT PRACTICE

This questionnaire should be completed with CIPFA's *Statements on Internal Audit Practice – Public Sector* in mind. The page numbers refer to the pages in the statements issued in July 1979.

1. *Organisation and staffing*

	19..	19..	19..	19..	
1.1 (*a*) Staff numbers. (*b*) Previous year's audit fee (£). (*c*) Amount of fee per auditor (£).					

1.2 Name, designation, grading and qualifications of the head of internal audit. ....

1.3 To whom is he directly responsible? ....

	Yes	No	Comments
1.4 Has the complement of internal audit been reviewed in relation to the requirements of the CIPFA statements on internal audit practice? If so, show numbers decided upon for professionally qualified staff; other experienced staff, trainee staff, clerical support staff. Record numbers in post as at .... (Attach a copy of the organisation chart.)			PQ . . OE . . T . . C . . PQ . . OE . . T . . C . .

	Yes	*No*	*Comments*
1.5 How many members of the internal audit staff are experienced in: (*a*) The review of the security of the computer installation? (*b*) Participating in computer systems and program development? (*c*) The review of procedural controls (live systems)? (*d*) The review of acquisition/leasing of computer equipment? (*e*) The use of computer resources? (*f*) Computer interrogation? Reference should be made to the detailed computer audit assessment.			
2. *Role and independence (pages 4, 6 & 7)*			
Statement: 'Internal audit must be sufficiently independent to enable the auditor to perform his duties in a manner which will allow his professional judgements and recommendations to be effective and impartial.'			
2.1 Have the responsibilities and rights of internal audit been clearly defined? (Attach a copy.)			
2.2 Do the responsibilities adequately reflect the requirements on page 4 of the CIPFA statements on internal audit practice? (Specify the shortcomings.)			

	Yes	*No*	*Comments*
2.3 Has the auditor direct access to the following when he considers such action necessary: (*a*) All departmental heads? (*b*) The chief executive? (*c*) Members of the management board?			
2.4 Confirm that the section takes no part in operating financial systems. If there are operational duties, give details (see also para. 4.4).			
2.5 Can the auditor: (*a*) Require production of any document or record? (*b*) See any goods or property? (*c*) Obtain information or explanation from any member of staff as he considers necessary?			
2.6 Do the enquiries confirm that there is nothing to impair the independence of the head of internal audit? (Examples on page 7 of the CIPFA statements.)			
2.7 Do the enquiries confirm there is nothing to impair the independence of audit team leaders in relation to their areas of responsibility? (See page 7 of the CIPFA statements.)			
3. *Due professional care (pages 7 & 8)*			
Statement: 'The auditor shall exercise due professional care in carrying out his duties.'			
3.1 Is a continuing overall review of the organisation's activities carried out by: (*a*) The head of internal audit? (*b*) Team leaders?			

Yes	No	Comments

Are the sources of information complete?

Note: This should include items such as:

(i) Council, committee and sub-committee minutes.
(ii) Officers' reports to committees.
(iii) Changes to internal control systems.
(iv) Notifications of staff appointments and terminations.
(v) Evidence of possible irregularities or fraud (see also para. 5.2).
(vi) Error reports produced by the computer.
(vii) Lists of debts to be written off.

3.2 Is there evidence that, on completion of each section of audit work, it is reviewed internally for quality control?

(Questions in other sections of this questionnaire also relate to this section.)

4. *Internal control (pages 9–11)*

Statement: 'Internal audit shall review the soundness, adequacy and application of internal controls, both financial and otherwise.'

4.1 Are the major systems of financial and other management controls:

(*a*) Fully documented?
(*b*) Periodically reviewed? (Indicate the period.)
(*c*) Periodically tested? (Indicate the period.)

If reviews or tests are partial only, state omissions.

	Yes	No	Comments
4.2 Are system weaknesses, when identified: (*a*) Evaluated as to the possible effect? (*b*) Investigated to ascertain whether a loss has been sustained as a result? (*c*) Remedied?			
4.3 Does the audit as practised provide adequately for: (*a*) Regularity testing? (*b*) Monitoring of management performance? (For example, management's adherence to, and achievement of, policy objectives and the efficient use of staff and other resources. (See the section on management control on page 10 of the CIPFA statements.)			
4.4 What proportions of audit man-days are spent on: (*a*) Audit duties? (*b*) Other duties and lost time? (See also para. 2.4.)			
4.5 Is there evidence of an adequate *current* audit (including site visits) of capital works by: (*a*) DLO? (*b*) Contract? Show the time allocated and the number and value of schemes, or comment on the standard of audit tests.			
5. *Irregularities and fraud (pages 11–12)*			
Statement: 'The internal auditor shall endeavour to reveal any serious defect in systems of internal control which might lead to the perpetration of fraud, and must have regard to the possibility of malpractice in areas under examination. He shall be alert to the			

Yes	No	Comments

possibility of corruption and be prepared to inform the appropriate level of management of any justifiable suspicions.'

5.1 Have procedures been laid down by management as to the action to be taken when there is prima facie evidence of irregularities or fraud?
Do they include guidance as to when the police are informed?

5.2 Is there an instruction to management at all levels to notify the head of internal audit of any suspicion/evidence of fraud or corruption?

5.3 Is the head of internal audit required to investigate all such notifications and any other similar information received?

5.4 Is there evidence that this responsibility has been adequately performed?

6. *Planning and control of audits (pages 13–14)*

Statement: 'Internal audit work must be planned and controlled in order to achieve the agreed objectives of the internal audit department, to establish audit priorities and to ensure the effective use of audit resources.'

6.1 Is there a long-term plan which provides adequate audit cover of all the organisation's activities:
(*a*) Regarding regularity auditing?
(*b*) Regarding management performance?

6.2 Is the cover related to a risk index?
If not, is it based upon some other assessment of known problems and areas of risk?

	Yes	*No*	*Comments*
6.3 Is the long-term plan reconciled to a realistic assessment of the staff available and a determined period of time?			
6.4 Is there a short-term plan designed to meet the needs of the long-term plan?			
6.5 Do long- and short-term plans record: (*a*) The work done by the external auditor? (*b*) The work he has undertaken to do?			
6.6 Is there evidence that, on completion of each section of audit work, it is reviewed in terms of objectives met and man-days allocated as a check on the validity of the audit plans? (See also para. 7.5.)			
6.7 Are the plans revised to allow for: (*a*) Changes in audit staff? (*b*) Changes in financial systems or personnel? (*c*) Other changes in the audit requirement? (For example, increased or reduced level of services.)			
6.8 Will the plans be fulfilled within a foreseeable period of time? (Compare this period with that originally determined at para. 6.3.)			
6.9 Does the head of internal audit report periodically the section's: (*a*) Objectives? (*b*) Resources? (*c*) Requirements? (*d*) Achievements? To whom does he make his report?			

Question	Yes	No	Comments
7. *Supervision (page 15)*			
Statement: 'Supervision during the preparation, conduct and closure of an internal audit is fundamental to effective audit practice.'			
7.1 Do records show that head of internal audit has agreed with his team leaders: (*a*) The areas to be covered? (*b*) The objectives? (*c*) The methods, scope and depth of tests?			
7.2 Are there written job instructions from team leaders to staff stating: (*a*) The area to be covered? (*b*) The objectives? (*c*) The methods, scope and depth of tests?			
7.3 Is the work done by internal audit well enough documented to enable its extent and depth to be assessed?			
7.4 Is there evidence of current supervision of the work of: (*a*) The team leaders by the head of internal audit? (*b*) The staff by their team leaders?			
7.5 Is there evidence that the man-days allocated to audits are controlled by: (*a*) The authorisation of significant variation to objectives, methods or audit tests? (*b*) The comparison of actual time with budgeted time? (See also para. 6.6.)			

	Yes	*No*	*Comments*

7.6 When was the work of the internal audit section last reviewed by an employee senior to the head of internal audit?
What prompted the review?
Who carried it out?
To whom did he report?
Did the review include:
(*a*) An examination of the organisation?
(*b*) An examination of methods?
(*c*) An examination of the records and files?

8. *Training (page 16)*

Statement: 'An internal auditor must be properly trained to fulfil his responsibilities.'

8.1 Is a training programme prepared for each inexperienced recruit to the audit section?

8.2 Does it provide for:
(*a*) Initial instruction in basic principles?
(*b*) Practical training?

8.3 Is specialist training provided for staff with general audit experience in:
(*a*) Computer audit?
(*b*) The audit of incentive bonus schemes?
(*c*) The audit of capital works?
(*d*) Any other specialism? (Specify.)

8.4 Is there liaison with the external auditor for training purposes?
If so, does this include attendance at common courses?
By whom and how frequently are they arranged?
(See also para. 11.1(h).)

Yes	No	Comments

9. *Evidence (pages 17–18)*

Statement: 'The internal auditor must have adequate and relevant evidence on which to base his conclusions and recommendations.'

9.1 Do the following records demonstrate, from the following, that sufficient evidence has been obtained to enable a professional judgement to be formed?
  (*a*) The extent of audit tests.
  (*b*) Their validity.
  (*c*) The persons who made the enquiries.
  (*d*) The persons who reviewed the findings.

10. *Reporting (pages 18–20)*

Statement: 'The findings and recommendations arising from an internal audit must be promptly conveyed to management.'

10.1 Are audit findings discussed with line management before the issue of formal reports?

10.2 Are written reports on matters of consequence issued by the head of internal audit under his own name and without editing?

10.3 Are they issued to:
  (*a*) Heads of departments? (Specify exceptions.)
  (*b*) The director of finance?
  (*c*) A chief executive?
  Are they issued promptly?

10.4 Do the reports:
  (*a*) State the scope, purpose and areas covered?
  (*b*) Enable the management to understand them and assess their value quickly?

	Yes	No	Comments
(*c*) Show that they are based upon relevant facts and are well documented?			
(*d*) Take account of the views expressed by line management?			
(*e*) Draw conclusions?			
(*f*) Make recommendations?			
10.5 Are recipients obliged to respond to recommendations in audit reports?			
10.6 Is there evidence that:			
(*a*) Changes follow reports?			
(*b*) Reports are followed up by a subsequent audit review?			
11. *Relationship with external audit (page 21)*			
Statement: 'The relationship with the external auditor should be based on an understanding of his role and on a degree of co-operation, including the exchange of relevant information sufficient to maximise audit performance.'			
11.1 Do relationships between internal and external audit extend to:			
(*a*) Frequent meetings?			
(*b*) The co-ordination of the audit plan?			
(*c*) Co-operation in ensuring that records of financial systems are kept up to date?			
(*d*) Testing financial systems?			
(*e*) The interchange of reports and discussion notes?			
(*f*) The immediate notification of frauds and other serious happenings?			
(*g*) A willingness to undertake joint enquiries into:			
(i) Irregularities?			
(ii) Other matters?			
(*h*) Co-operation in staff training. (See also para. 8.4.)			

Yes	No	Comments

12. *Relationships with client departments and with other review agencies (pages 21–23)*

Statement: 'The relationship between the internal auditor and the management and staff of the departments subject to audit must be based on mutual confidence and understanding.'

Statement: 'The internal auditor's relationship with other review agencies must be based on mutual confidence and understanding, but must not compromise the relationship between the auditor and the client department.'

12.1 Is there evidence that internal audit is not accepted in any client departments? (Specify these departments, if any.)

12.2 Does liaison with management services provide for:

(*a*) The discussion of MSU findings with internal audit before the issue of reports if they affect internal control?

(*b*) The discussion of internal audit findings with MSU before the issue of reports if they affect management control systems?

(*c*) Regular meetings between internal audit and MSU to discuss their plans and assignments?

(*d*) Joint assignments?

12.3 Is internal audit involved in performance review committee projects?
If so, in what way?

Index